The World
of

PERCY
FRENCH

The World

of

PERCY FRENCH

by

BRENDAN O'DOWDA

music copyist
Elizabeth Bicker

THE
BLACKSTAFF PRESS
BELFAST

ACKNOWLEDGEMENTS

My thanks, for their help, to the Misses Ettie and Joan French, Alan Tongue, Frank O'Dowda, Mrs Claire French, John Riddell and John McKenna.

Cartoons by Rowel Friers reproduced by kind permission of Mr Friers and the BBC.

First published in 1981 by
The Blackstaff Press Limited
3 Galway Park, Dundonald, Belfast BT16 0AN, Northern Ireland
Reprinted 1982; with additional material, 1991

Printed by The Guernsey Press Company Limited
British Library Cataloguing in Publication Data
O'Dowda, Brendan
The world of Percy French.
1. French, Percy 2. Authors, Irish – 20th Century
– Biographies
I. Title
784.4'9415'0924   PR6011.R45Z/
ISBN 0-85640-482-9

CONTENTS

PREFACE

'Nobody,' says Dr Johnson, 'can write the life of a man, but those who have eat and drunk and lived in social intercourse with him.'

Since I myself wasn't born till some years after the death of Percy French, I make no apologies for quoting liberally from family, friends, contemporaries and critics, for these were the people who really did know him. Of inestimable help has been my twenty years of friendship with his two talented daughters Ettie and Joan. Their guidance and assistance in granting me access to personal and otherwise unavailable material was invaluable. I now feel I have got to know him maybe even better than many a close contemporary. I say this because I firmly believe that any one acquaintance only saw that side of the man which applied to him or her. I am left with a strong image of a man of contradictions.

He was a child at heart who loved nothing better than to romp with youth, yet he revelled in the intellectual discourse. He wanted very much to be a success as an artist, composer and entertainer, yet he had absolutely no comprehension of the value of money or dress sense. The greatest contradiction of all was in his social life. In an age when lines of social demarcation were very emphatically defined, he straddled them regardless.

He was a product of the 'the Big House' and the Irish landed gentry; reared with the luxury of governesses, servants and tutors and educated in the best schools and colleges. On his countless tours of Ireland he would only rarely stay in hotels, preferring the hospitality of the local 'manor house', where he happily rubbed shoulders with such celebrities as Lord Kitchener. While one foot rested happily in that land, his other was firmly implanted in the realm of the Irish country folk for whom he had an unquestionable love, for they were a part of the scenery that for him was incomparable, and he revelled in their company.

On the other hand, while he lived and mingled with his Irish aristocratic equals, he was to write about their English counterparts, 'these people and I have nothing in common . . .'

Yet another enigma I find is his endless wanderlust on the one hand and his utter devotion to his home, wife and children on the other. Judging by the painstaking and lengthy letters to his wife and three daughters individually, he was more attentive, concerned and loving than anyone I have known. Maybe some psychologist could analyse this apparently simple yet intricate character much better, but in all my research I am left with one overriding impression that here was a man who, irrespective of whatever social path he trod, was a very loving and tender person, deeply and sincerely loved by everyone (and I really do mean everyone) with whom he came into contact. Nowhere, in either the written or spoken word, have I found an atom of evidence to the contrary. His only sin seems to have been a neglect of self.

This then is the outline of his life with some samples of what made up 'The World of Percy French'.

Percy French's daughters, Ettie and Joan, with Brendan O'Dowda.

NOTE TO THE 1991 EDITION

I never cease to be amazed at the universal depth of love and interest shown for Percy French and his work, especially when it emanates from the most unlikely sources. When I perform in places like Hong Kong, Singapore, New Zealand and Australia, there are always letters awaiting me requesting his songs, and two incidents are, I think, worthy of special note.

While performing some four years ago in Loyola University, New Orleans, a professor there gave me a copy of a book on James Joyce – no mean tenor in his own right – and therein was an entire chapter entitled 'The Influence on Joyce of Percy French', emphasising Joyce's admiration for French's talent, with liberal quotes from the former's works and containing typical Joycean puns such as 'Come back baddy wrily' and so on.

A more unusual thing happened in Dublin when John McKeon from Clonskeagh met me after a show at the Olympia. He was a retired barrister who had practised in Lusaka, Zambia, for many years. There he had met a Father P.J. O'Brien, who loved the songs of Percy French. However, the only language understood by all multinational members of Church and legal circles there was Latin. So, inspired by another priest, they translated into Latin the chorus and three verses of 'Phil the Fluter's Ball'. Eventually we made contact and I was able to send him a private recording of my effort. I am assured by Latin scholars that Father O'Brien's is a most erudite work, as it contains a comprehensive glossary of well-nigh every word in the song. I met him when, because of ill health, he returned to Dublin two years ago. He died there earlier this year, and I will always remember him as one of the kindliest and most loving people I have ever been acquainted with. Herewith is the first verse and chorus:

DE CHOREA TIBICINIS PHILIPPI

De Tibicine Philippo audivistis-ne adhuc?
Egestas pressit eum, habitavit Ballymuck.
Ergo suis scripsit proximis: 'Propono vespere
Choream celebrare, ad quam nunc invite te.'
Nec dum invitabat oblitus est suggerere,
Quod si viderunt petasum, vicinum ad portam,
Quanto plus pecuniae voluerint inserere
Eo melius posset ipsemet sonare musicam.

CHORUS

Fit strepitus a tibia et crepitus fidicula,
In medio saltatur, sicus piscis in craticula.
Sursum, deorsum usque ad moenia.
Hilaritas praestabat in Philippi chorea.

BRENDAN O'DOWDA

OCTOBER 1991

The Life of
PERCY FRENCH

by
Brendan O'Dowda

The French family tree in my possession begins with one Jeffry French of Mulpit, Co. Galway, who died there in 1610. The ensuing generations seem to have contributed either a High Sheriff to Roscommon or even more likely, a Major General serving in Europe, the West Indies or America. A particularly colourful character was a certain Christopher, who in the early 1740s was stationed in Minorca with the 22nd Regiment. He fell in love with a young beauty he had seen through the gates of a convent. Several clandestine meetings followed, with the young lovers always divided by the 'holy grille'. Eventually, with the aid of a fellow soldier, who had, it seems, also formed a liaison with another of the students, they got both maidens out of the convent window and straight to a church where they were married. Christopher's wife Margarita Alberti survived him by only five months after almost fifty years of blissful marriage. Her name is kept alive by one of the family, happily still fit and well – Maeve Alberti French, otherwise Mrs Kenny of Ballinrobe – whose extremely talented son Courtney is a dear friend of mine and often an indispensible partner in my stage work.

In 1851 another Christopher, High Sheriff of Roscommon and Doctor of Law, married Susan Emma, daughter of the Rev. William Alex Percy, Rector of Kiltoghert, Co. Leitrim. This was the same Percy family which was to produce one of Ireland's most illustrious Olympic champions, Bob Tisdall. As the eldest son of the family, Christopher inherited their estate at Cloonyquin, between Elphin and Tulsk, in Co. Roscommon.

In these remote and beautiful surroundings their nine children, four boys and five girls, were to spend a happy and carefree childhood. History surrounded them. From the steps of Cloonyquin House could be seen Rathcroghan, the ancient burial place of the Kings of Connaught and beneath which, it is said, the palace of Queen Maeve lies buried. Also on their estate lay Lissoy, the family home of the Goldsmiths. In his life of Goldsmith, John Francis Waller states that Oliver was born on 10 November 1728 at Pallas on the banks of the river Inny in Co. Westmeath, the family moving to Lissoy, about three

1

miles from Ballymahon, a few years later. A footnote of further interest in his book says that Oliver's mother's family (she had been born in Elphin) maintain that 'he was born at Ardnegown in Roscommon, his grandfather Jones' house. Mr Joseph Goldsmith, the poet's greatgrand-nephew writes to me ['me' being J.F. Waller] (February 20th 1864) "the late James Lloyd who lived at Smith Hills near Elphin told me that Oliver was born in his house." He had the information from their common grandmother'.

On 1 May 1854 William Percy French was born into a close, contented and active family. Remotely situated as they were, it was necessary to import tutors and governesses, at various times, but the excellent library maintained by their father seemed to have contributed even more to their education. The first literary aspirations were realised in their own family magazine 'The Tulsk Morning Howl' and later 'The Trombone of Truth'. Percy was editor, his sisters contributed poetry, while cousins and friends added various items. But mostly it was Percy's poems, stories and drawings. His sister Emily Lucy, later Mrs DeBurgh Daly, lamented in her excellent book *Chronicles and Poems of Percy French* that

> It was curious that my father, who was extremely proud of his son's cleverness, never realised that all this pointed to more than mere talent. He was a very intellectual man, a capital classical scholar and very keen on giving his children a good education. But it did not dawn on him that Percy's artistic talents should have received special encouragement and development.

Cloonyquin House, Co. Roscommon: painting by Percy French.

Meanwhile Percy enjoyed his idyllic surroundings where his fertile imagination, which was to prove such an asset, had full range.

In my boyhood days my sole object in life was to see how little I could learn and how much I could idle. Looking back on those peaceful days, it seems that nowhere in the world were there more pleasant meadows, more mysterious underwoods or lovelier flowers than at old Cloonyquin. My first and only attempt to murder my father took place when I was five years old. The facts are these. My father, one of the best and kindest of men, had called me 'fatty' before a grown-up visitor. These were the words that sealed his doom! I was 'fat', very fat, but no one should call me 'fatty' in public and live. Quivering with rage, I ran out of the room and seizing my wooden spade, I strode forth across the lawn, and in the gloomy depths of a Portugal laurel I dug a pit. Deep and wide it seemed to me then, and well suited for the destruction of an offending parent, for in the centre of the pit I planted a sharpened stick, point upwards. Then I went into the garden and moodily ate gooseberries till the dinner bell rang. The reasons why my father did not die a lingering death impaled on the pointed stake are two in number. In the first place the hole cannot have been more than a foot deep; and secondly no one ever used that laurel as a thoroughfare, except myself.

A very diminutive stream (so small that in some places it was entirely arched over by long grasses and ferns), ran through one of the home meadows. In some remote age, possibly my father's boyhood, some beneficent being had caused the banks of the stream to be widened and a stone dam to be built across its course. There have been greater feats of engineering carried out since then, but no excavations or retaining walls ever gave such joy to the heart of a small boy as the expansion of that little stream.

What pageants have passed before me on that beloved pond! Hanno the Carthaginian has sailed forth without chart or compass over that unknown sea. On those placid waters the Spanish Armada, pushed off by Philip II in person, has gone forth to its doom! Columbus, lashed to the mast of a clockwork steamer, has peered anxiously across that watery waste, and on that shore the great Napoleon Bonaparte, his flat-bottomed fleet awaiting a favourable breeze, has moodily eaten bread and jam, while scowling at the dim coast that was never to own his sway.

I dwell on those early years for they were, I firmly believe, truly formative. In those last paragraphs I can see the birth of an imagination that was to give us such mock epics as 'Slattery's Mounted Fut', 'The Mary Ann McHugh' and 'Andy McElroe'.

By this time the French estate was becoming run-down and it was obvious that this third child would eventually have to go out into the world and earn his own living. For educational purposes part of the family moved to Derby where Willie (as Percy was always known to those close to him) attended Kirk Langley School and later Windermere College. In the early 1870s we find him at Foyle College in Derry getting a final 'grinding' for the Trinity College entrance examination.

My tutor at Foyle built up a beautiful superstructure on the flimsiest foundation and in 1872 I passed into TCD with honours. Here was a chance to learn everything! lectures by specialists of world-wide fame, a magnificent library, quiet rooms in the new square, debating societies, aspiring students all around me – yet nothing I wanted to know. Oh! yes there was! The Gaiety Theatre had just been opened – night after night I was in the pit – music held me in its magic spell – so I bought a banjo.

At one point in his education Percy had shown a certain aptitude for Euclid and 'those fatal honours in mathematics had confirmed my father in the belief that some day I would show Edison up as the Village Idiot, and a civil engineer I had to be'.

I believe I still hold the record as the student who took the longest time to get the CE Degree. Bright-eyed boys would pass through the school and get lucrative posts in various parts of the world, returning years after, bronzed and bearded men, to find me still attending Apjohn's lectures on the Skew Arch. I think taking up the banjo, lawn tennis and water-colour painting instead of Chemistry, Geology and the theory of strains, must have retarded my progress a good deal.

Percy French (with banjo) with his cousin Johnny Richardson.

Not unexpectedly, he was soon an integral part of the social life of Trinity, ever ready to entertain at parties and 'smokers'. This was in spite of the fact that then and all through his life he was most abstemious. He explains, 'luckily for me, a natural dislike of alcohol in every form, an inability to smoke without being violently sick, and a tendency to forget what were trumps at whist, kept me out of the society of the more Rackety Botany Babes'. So you can evaluate what credence can be lent to those stories of his frequenting the pubs of Ireland. Years later in Cavan he even gave temperance lectures, using his own drawings for the purpose. For instance, the drinker shown at the sea's edge – then further in and then deeper, until the 'Sea of Liquor' closes over his head!

It was for one of those same 'smokers' in 1877 that he wrote his first song 'Abdallah - Bulbul Ameer', of which one magazine wrote, 'It has sounded in the Australian outbacks, in the diamond mines of South Africa; on the cattle trails of the West and on the decks of Arctic trawlers. The undignified and unforgettable air has been whistled in Chicago poolrooms, in the water dives of Marseilles and in every pub from Fairbanks to Hobart'. Yet Percy French was never to receive a penny of royalties.

Some years later he explained.

I decided to publish. To borrow a fiver from my friend Archie West, the only man of means in my class, was the work of a moment, and when Messrs Cramer & Co. handed me two hundred copies to be disposed of at 1/6d. a copy, Eldorado seemed round the corner. But alas! we had forgotten to take out the copyright, and a London firm, finding out our mistake, brought out a pirated edition without even my name on the cover. As they had taken care to copyright their version, I was tricked out of all rights to my song, though words and music were both mine.

It wasn't until he had met Dublin publisher John Pigott some years later, when a close and lasting association was formed, that his faith in human nature, and publishers in general, was restored. More recently I was personally involved in rekindling the sleeping embers of his discontent with the aforesaid London publishers. Faced with the weight of evidence, they conceded the inevitable, and Percy French was duly re-enrolled as the indisputed author. I like to think that when he looked down and viewed this piece of justice being done, he gave a little chuckle of satisfaction.

At Trinity he scorned the rules on late nights and could often be seen in the early hours of the morning scaling the high gates in Brunswick Street with his banjo slung over his back. His closest friend Archie West shared with him in purchasing a piano and when Percy's father unexpectedly came to visit them in their college rooms, they both donned their gowns and draped themselves in front of the piano for the duration of the visit. Percy was afraid his father would deem it an unnecessary extravagance. The camouflage proved a success, helped not a little by his father's short-sightedness.

He describes his farewell to Trinity – 'eventually I was allowed to take out my BA and CE degrees. I believe the Board were afraid I should apply for a pension if I stayed any longer at TCD'.

He served his apprenticeship with James Price, engineer-in-chief of the Midland Railway, where he found a common bond with a fellow apprentice, Charles Manners. There was little work and both spent most of their days rehearsing duets to banjo and bones accompaninent. This was the same Charles Manners who was to become world renowned as a superb operatic bass and who in later years, with his wife Fanny Moody, established the popular Moody-Manners Opera Company.

In the year 1881 however, it was the 'Manners-French' combine, and they decided to put their act to the test in public. Since no offers were forthcoming from any of the Dublin theatres, they decided to entertain the racegoers at Punchestown race course. They got to Kingsbridge (now Heuston) Station on the appointed day with their banjo, bones and small bags. Slipping into an empty room they changed, blackened up their faces and as Christie Minstrels boarded the train, where they endeavoured to entertain the passengers.

Inevitably both their stories varied. As Percy seemed to revel in self-effacement he maintained they were heckled on the train journey as they didn't have any music-hall songs in their repertoire, while the people at the course thought them 'too vulgar for words'. His final scene was of the stage-struck pair washing the burnt cork off their faces in a muddy stream and dividing their net eightpence profit with all due ceremony.

On the other hand, Charles Manners' memories of the day were somewhat less discouraging. He maintained that they were well received and had good fun performing for people they knew extremely well but who didn't recognise them beneath their make-up. A ragged old ballad singer and his twelve-year-old daughter approached them

6

with an offer of a partnership which they declined, while a party insisted on their playing for them for over an hour, resulting in their getting back to College some twenty-eight shillings to the better.

'The *Mary Ann McHugh*':
cartoon by Rowel Friers

It was in 1881 that he got the offer of a post as an 'Inspector of Loans to Tenants' with the Cavan Board of Works. Years later he wrote,

> £300 per year and travelling expenses were untold wealth to a bachelor boy. So having bought a new set of banjo strings and a tennis racquet, I set off to take up my duties. We were paid nine pence a mile for travelling and fifteen shillings for hotel expenses, and since I always used a bicycle and stopped at a friend's house, this added considerably to one's income. Now of all my private hotels, few pleasanter ones were there than the Rev. James Godley's rectory at Carrigallen, Co Leitrim.

Soon he was almost a part of the Godley family and it was on one of those visits that an incident occurred which inspired one of his most famous songs. This is how he recounted it:

> One evening the Rev. James Godley came in after one of his long walks and told me how he had met the local flute player and how he had paid his rent.
>
> 'I've paid up all me arrears, yer riverence', said Phil the Fluter – for, as my readers have already surmised, 'twas himself that was in it.
>
> 'And how did you manage that?' said his reverence.
>
> 'I give a ball', said Phil.
>
> 'A ball!' said his reverence. 'If my family asked me to give a ball, I'd have to put my hand in my pocket, and I think I'd keep it there,' he added thoughtfully.
>
> 'Well,' said Phil. 'You'd make a hole in a couple o' pound givin' your ball, for you'd have a young lady to play the pianna and cake and sandwidges an' other combustibles. Now when I give a ball, I clean out me cabin and lock up any food or drink in the cupboard. Then I put me hat behind the door; the neighbours come in bringin' their suppers wid them, and each puttin' a shillin' or two in the hat. Then I cock me leg over the dresser, throw me top lip over the flute and toother away like a hatful o' larks and there they stay leppin' like hares till two in the mornin'.'

And so was born this inimitable character and all those colourful individuals who had patronised his now famous 'ball'. Personally I owe much to this particular song. Like many another budding trained tenor, I lived in the world of opera and the 'better' Irish songs. It was not until I had been a professional for some years, that a musician, of whose work I thought highly, remarked to me, after I had been bulldozed into including it on a TV show, 'You know, if I were to die tomorrow and could be remembered for one song — if that song was "Phil the Fluter", then I'd rest happy'.

I thought the man to be mad, as I had seen and heard fellows rolling home drunk and yelling out the self-same ballad. Not until he pointed out to me what an excellent musical word-picture it was, did I see the light. Little did I realise then that some years later I would be singing it, under the baton of Eric Robinson, accompanied by the full might of the Liverpool Philharmonic Orchestra. That experience whetted my appetite and from it grew my interest in Percy French.

When one of the Godley family wrote to him in verse re his 'appointment to the sewers of Cavan', a lengthy swapping of verse continued over a period, culminating in his self-satirical 'Inspector of Drains'. These years in Cavan were seemingly the happiest and certainly the most important in his life. Always a very active person, he bought a bicycle which, apart from its use in work, conveyed him far and wide on his other pursuits of tennis, hockey and even fencing. In tennis he won several prizes in major tournaments and retained a life-time interest in the game.

The colourful rural characters he met or heard about in his ceaseless wanderings rekindled his interest in verse and songwriting, which had been justifiably soured since his unfortunate experience with 'Abdul'. From those years in Cavan, apart from the two pieces already mentioned, came 'Andy McElroe' and 'Slattery's Mounted Fut', amongst others. His rustic ramblings also re-awoke his love of water-colour painting and this pursuit was, before long, consuming much of his spare time. He even managed to start a sketching club (just one of several he was to start in Ireland) and with the collaboration of some equally enthusiastic locals, devised an amateur minstrel company, The Kinnypottle Komics, a title inspired by the little Kinnypottle stream which flowed through the town of Cavan. While his entertaining and artistic efforts seemed to be in demand and much appreciated, the efforts of the Board of Works and their not very enthusiastic employee were not always well received. One old rustic remarked to him, 'It's ruinin' the country wid drainage you are. Shure there's not a fat shnipe to be got in these parts now, where there used to be whisps o' them wheelin' round ye like catamarans!!'

By now Percy was in his thirties and no great love, let alone marriage, had managed to lure him from his bohemian bachelor independence. Towards the end of that decade, however, the scene altered considerably, for he fell in love with the very beautiful and petite Ethel Kathleen Armytage Moore, to whom he always referred as his 'Little Ray of Sunshine'. He had met her at a tennis party in the home of a Dr Mease. Friends there remembered him as 'fat and jolly' and maintained it was Ettie's mother who initially set her cap at him – but he obviously had other ideas. The family came from Arnmore and Ettie was the sister of the Countess Annesley, who lived, I believe, at Castlewellan, Co. Down.

When Donal Giltinan, playwright and author of the very successful musical on Percy French *The Golden Years*, visited Cavan some years after the troubadour's death, he collected interesting anecdotes from some contemporaries. One man who was then living in Percy's old house told of a door with the four panels decorated with oil paintings. This was borne out by a local house-painter, a Mr Gordon, who told of being instructed by various tenants to 'paint around' the works of art. He said that, in addition to the landscapes, there were 'corner pieces, with frogs and birds and so on'. A Robert Carson, who lived next door to Percy in Farnham Street, said that in his 'office' he saw, in addition to the few official documents on a table, such things as a banjo in one corner and easels, paints and canvasses in another; pictures painted on the backs of doors and his autograph engraved on a window-pane.

Several remembered the episode of the street banjo-player who stopped to play outside Percy's window – only to be invited in, by the occupier, for an evening's refreshment and banjo duets. This hospitality so impressed the strolling player that he once stayed on in Cavan for several weeks. Another local told of being invited to tea years later to Percy's home in Mespil Road, Dublin, where conversation was rendered difficult through the constant noise made by two other gents, practising with foils across the room. Most agreed that his job was often in jeopardy because of his bohemianism.

Illustration for *The Jarvey* by Ettie French, Percy French's first wife.

10

THE JARVEY

No. 80] SATURDAY, JULY 19, 1890. [PRICE ONE PENNY.

HARD TO COMPLY WITH.

PRISON KEEPER.—" You will have to work here, Moriarty, but you may select any trade you wish.'

PRISONER. "Well, if it's all the same to you, sor, oi'd like to be a sailor."

Cover page of *The Jarvey*,
19 July 1890.

11

Even his best friend could never have accused Percy of being over-absorbed in his job of 'Inspector of Drains'. So when the Board of Works was reducing its staff, he was unceremoniously given the sack. Any money he had managed to save he had invested in a distillery, which most inconveniently contrived to go into liquidation at about the same time. Prior to this he had been, for several years, successfully submitting humorous prose and verse to *The Irish Cyclist*, which was just one of the many periodicals emanating from the Middle Abbey Street, Dublin, offices of Mecredy & Kyle. So he called on the editor R.J. Mecredy and asked for a permanent post. R.J. went one better and offered to make him editor of a brand new weekly comic paper to be called *The Jarvey* – grandiosely advertised as 'The Irish Punch'. He admitted knowing nothing about the actual running of a paper, and the owner's policy of no initial capital, with artists and writers being paid out of the monthly profits, held out little hope of survival. He later lamented, 'at the end of the first month there were no profits; at the end of the second month there were no writers or artists, except my very good friends, Dick Orpen and Eddy Radcliffe'.

Having read through every edition, I feel he should also have added Ettie, whose fine drawings figured prominently in almost every 1890 copy. The first edition reached the news-stands on 3 January 1889, to a varied reception. Typically he remembered only one adverse comment, from *The Freeman's Journal*: 'We have before us the first number of a journal devoted to art and humour. Some of the jokes we've seen before – some we haven't seen yet!!!' His childhood nickname of 'Willy Wagtail' concealed his own identity in innumerable contributions.

Family and friends always stressed his lack of interest in 'time' – never dating letters and forgetting appointments. Since researching, my name can be added to the list. For instance, he maintained he married his 'Little Ray of Sunshine' on the strength of his income as editor of *The Jarvey* and as I just mentioned, financial problems had already presented themselves by the end of February 1889. He must however have still been very hopeful by 28 June 1890, for it was on that date they married at St Stephen's Parish Church (C. of I.), Dublin, eighteen

Illustration for *The Jarvey* by Percy French.

"WHEN THE HUSBANDS HOMEWARD FLY."
SANDYMOUNT, 2 P.M. SATURDAY.

" Maria will be furious if I've forgotten anything."

12

THE JARVEY

THE IRISH PUNCH.

No. 94] SATURDAY, OCTOBER 25, 1890. [PRICE ONE PENNY.

IRATE CYCLIST—" Call off your dog, can't you !
MISS ALLTHAIR—" Come away, Sport, you silly dog ; these are not bones—these are the gentleman's legs.'

Printed and Published by the Sole Proprietors, MECREDY & KYLE, Middle Abbey Street, Dublin.

 J. M'KENNY, | ROYAL VETERINARY COLLEGE INFIRMARY | DUBLIN.
M.R.C.V.S. | 116, STEPHEN'S GREEN
Telegraphic Address. "VET." Dublin

Cover page of *The Jarvey,*
25 October 1890.

13

months after the first edition and just six months before the last.

It was a blissfully happy marriage, but in spite of their united efforts *The Jarvey* seemed doomed. In an interview given to the Dublin *Evening Telegraph* in 1892 he blamed its failure on several factors. He felt that 'the name was not a good one – barriers of prejudice had to be broken down, but the exchequer broke down first. But mainly it failed because it was impossible to get it pushed, as the local shopkeepers preferred inducing their customers to buy a London publication'. Typically, he coaxed it through its final issues with an air of humorous inevitability.

> The allotted life of a Dublin comic journal being two years, I was not altogether surprised when R.J. told me the Xmas number of 1890 would be our last. That expiring effort was a great one. I advertised that the number would consist of new and original stories and poems by all the great authors from Chaucer to Conan Doyle, and then set to work to write them myself! One of these, which Longfellow sent me, was the very last of Hiawatha's adventures: 'How Hiawatha played cricket'! but even that did not save the journal.

Poring through the issues of *The Jarvey* I noted how he had managed to keep one foot on land as he sailed the good ship *Jarvey*. Within months of its launching, he was using a full page to advertise 'The Jarvey Concert Company' – 'Grand series of concerts with Music, Mirth and Mystery!' Judging by the press notices of the time, the 'Company' consisted of Percy himself, Eddy Radcliffe and a Professor Leozedt, 'one of the deftest disciples of the great Houdini we have ever seen'. (*Lurgan Times*).

From August 1890 the columns of the journal were used by himself and Richard Orpen to announce the launching of their first book, *The First Lord Liftinant* – a typical satire of the Queen Elizabeth and Lord Essex saga. They followed it up with their own 'Press Opinions'. 'Invaluable as a pipe lighter' – 'Returned with many, many thanks' – 'a boon to the waste paper trade'. However, I myself find in it some of his funniest lines, and a certain 'goon-like' humour which must have seemed original in the early 1890s.

Never a one to prepare for the rainy day, the early months of 1891 were indeed hard for the unemployed Percy and his young, fragile and by now pregnant wife. By June her health was visibly failing and on the 29th, the day following their first wedding anniversary, his tender little Ettie died in childbirth. Their baby only survived a few weeks. This dual loss was heartbreaking, for as he worshipped his young wife, he loved children.

This latter trait was a dominant factor in his life, and in my opinion the secret of his especial mentality and talent. I believe that that wonderful imagination we all possess as children, but unfortunately

14

THE DEVIL.

On a winter's evening dreary, as I pondered
    worn and weary
Over many an ancient chestnut of the dismal
    days of yore ;
Suddenly I heard a tapping, as of some one
    gently rapping,
And there came a little chap in, who the
    name of " Devil' bore,
Who the name of " Printer's Devil," and the
    ghastly message bore—
       " Foreman wants a column more."

" What !" I cried," another column ?" and my
    face grew long and solemn,
And my voice no longer dulcet rose into a
    lion's roar ;
" I have got no jokes that gladden,
    Merely mildewed puns that madden ;
Let him shove a printing ' ad.' in,
    One that he has got in store."
" All the ' ads.'" replied the Devil,
" Have been measured in before—
    Still he wants a column more."

Then I pondered for a minute,
    How on earth should I begin it ;
But my head had nothing in it—
    Naught but jokes I'd told before ;
Nothing but the melancholy, mould-encrusted
    jokes of yore.
Suddenly I cried " Eureka !" why in fancy
    should I seek a
Subject when I have the Devil standing on
    my office floor,
When I have the very Devil standing on
    my office floor—
       Fill a column !– aye and more.

So I wrote what ye are reading ;
    Then into the darkness speeding,
Caught a passing tram which bore me to the wind-
    swept Merrion's shore ;
But still in my nightly dreaming,
    I could see two eye-balls gleaming,
And could hear a shrill voice screaming,
    As I'd heard it oft before—
       " Foreman wants a column more."

Page from *The Jarvey*, 27 December 1890: illustration by Ettie French, Percy French's first wife.

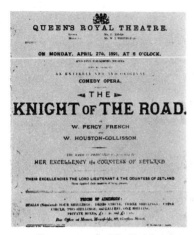

QUEEN'S ROYAL THEATRE.

ON MONDAY, APRIL 27th, 1891, AT 8 O'CLOCK.

AN ENTIRELY NEW AND ORIGINAL
COMEDY OPERA,

◄ THE ►
KNIGHT OF THE ROAD.

W. PERCY FRENCH
AND
W. HOUSTON-COLLISSON.

HER EXCELLENCY the COUNTESS OF ZETLAND

THEIR EXCELLENCIES THE LORD LIEUTENANT & THE COUNTESS OF ZETLAND

Programme for *The Knight of the Road.*

lose with maturity, was never lost to Percy French – but merely matured into his particular characteristic of being unable to take anything too seriously, often portraying it in a humorous vein.

> I was born a boy and have remained one ever since. Friends and relatives often urge me to grow up and take an interest in politics, whiskey, race meetings, foreign securities, poor rates, options and other things men talk about – but no! I am still the small boy messing about with a paint box, or amusing myself with pencil and paper, while fogies of forty determine the Kaiser's next move.

His poem 'Retrospection' expresses the same sentiments. One friend remembered him, only a few years before his untimely death, literally on all fours pursuing his host's little girls under tables and chairs.

That, then is the man, now bereft of wife and child. Earlier that same year he had collaborated with a William Houston Collisson, Mus. Doc., in writing a musical entitled *The Knight of the Road*, later re-named *The Irish Girl*. At that time Dr Collisson was a well-known figure in Irish music circles. An excellent pianist, accompanist and arranger, he regularly promoted concerts of considerable musical prestige.

On 27 April 1891, just two months before Ettie died, the curtain went up in the Queens Theatre, Dublin, on the first Irish musical comedy ever written.

> ...since the Doctor had Musical Societies, vocal and instrumental, at his beck and call, we soon had a fine chorus in full cry and an orchestra in full blast. Henry Beaumont, the Carl Rosa tenor and Miss Dubedat were the only paid professionals in the cast. We paid all expenses and also allowed the male chorus the run of the bar. The Irish drink bill went up that fortnight by leaps and bounds! However, we had packed houses every night and it gave us all a lovely time, putting £200 to my credit in the Bank of Ireland.

They reproduced it a short time later, during Horse Show week in fact, with 'full-house' notices. Acclaimed by press and public alike, they seemed on the threshold of success.

Later that year he teamed up with his talented friend Richard Orpen in writing *Dublin Up To Date*. This was a type of 'lantern-lecture' illustrated with caricatures of celebrities in and out of society. It was staged at the 'Antient Concert Rooms' and yet again was a great success. Richard had enlisted the services of his brother Willie and during the interval they contributed to the exchequer, by drawing lightning sketches in coloured chalks for the patrons, at a small fee. From this humble beginning Willie Orpen was to blossom forth into the very same Sir William Orpen, a painter of world acclaim. How many patrons, I wonder, in later years must have rued consigning their cheaply purchased drawings to the waste basket!

16

In 1892 the result of further collaboration with Dr Collisson came to fruition with the birth of another musical, *Strongbow*. Again it was staged in the Queens Theatre, starting in Easter week. This time however they had unthinkingly chosen a prickly subject. 'It is,' he wrote, 'a fine dramatic tale, but I was born without any sense of reverence for anything or anybody, and see the humorous side of things too plainly. So, in a moment of regrettable thoughtlessness I made a comic episode out of the conquest of Ireland by the English'. Although the reception this time left a lot to be desired, his reputation seemed in no way affected, for I have before me, by kind permission of his daughters, a 'Plan of Tables' for the 'Annual Dinner of the Incorporated Society of Authors: President – Lord Tennyson', dated 31 May 1892, where he is rubbing shoulders with such giants of the literary world as the poet William Allingham and authors H. Rider Haggard, Jerome K. Jerome, Conan Doyle and Oscar Wilde. He obviously wasn't one whit overawed, for he seemed to have spent much of the evening filling the blank areas of the plan with drawings of his fellow guests, among them an excellent side-view of Wilde who sat at an adjacent table.

Richard attended that dinner with his friend and Percy had found much comfort in his lonely life visiting the Orpen home in Blackrock, outside Dublin. He then decided to take their successful show *Dublin Up To Date* on tour, but Richard, by now a rising architect, could not travel, so he was forced to go it alone. His first show was very experimental but was a hit. He decided 'Yes! that mighty ovation told me that if there was no demand for me as an engineer I might yet succeed as an entertainer'. Gradually expanding with each appearance, his one-man show eventually comprised recitations, character sketches, and drawings used to illustrate particular stories, only to be inverted at the conclusion to show something utterly different. The musical contents were mainly his own compositions sung to a banjo accompaniment. Most of his best songs were written without any potential publication in mind, but rather as something new for his act. Their eventual publication was secondary and so many are lost, as they had never even reached the

Overleaf: Table Plan for the 1892 Annual Dinner of the Incorporated Society of Authors, complete with Percy French's character sketches.

17

VENETIAN ROOM,

Head Table (H):

No.	Name
27	Rev. William Hunt.
25	Thistleton Dyke, C.B.
23	H. Rider Haggard.
21	Andrew Lang.
19	R. L. Nettleship.
17	William Pole, F.R.S.
15	Sir John Evans, K.C.B.
13	Mrs. Lynn Linton.
11	G. Darwin, F.R.S.
9	Mrs. Darwin.
7	Austin Dobson.
5	Humphry Ward.
3	Prof. T. Huxley, F.R.S.
1	Mrs. Humphry Ward.

Table F (W. Morris Collis):

Name	No.	No.	Name	Name	No.
A. W. Dubourg.	11	12	Henry Harland.	"Daily News."	13
Rev. A. W. Mommerie	10	12a	Mrs. Mona Caird.	J. Theodore Bent.	12
Mr. Orpen.	9	13	Ashby Sterry.	Mackenzie Bell.	11
Mrs. Orpen.	8	14	C. T. C. James.	William Watson.	10
Charles Mercier.	7	15	W. O. Greener.	W. Baptiste Scoones.	9
Sir Randall Roberts	6	F 16	Trevor Battye.	H. R. Tedder.	8
Comtesse de Bremont	5	17	J. T. Grein.	Rev. Charles Voysey.	7
J. D. Hutcheson.	4	18	Robert Ross.	A. G. Ross.	6
		10a	Oscar Wilde.	Miss Loftie.	5
Mrs. Hutcheson.	4a	19	G. W. Sheldon.	S. S. Sprigge.	4
Thos. Catling.	3	20	Jerome K. Jerome.	Basil Field.	3
Conan Doyle.	2	21	Mrs. Collis.	Dr. Sisley.	2

W. Morris Collis.

Table D (Rev. Middleton Wake):

No.	Name	Name	No.
14	John B. Crozier.	"Standard."	12
15	Dr. Bridges.	William Allingham.	11
16	James Baker.	J. M. Lely.	10
17	Clive Holland.	Egerton Castle.	9
18	Mrs. Cox.	Miss K. Beaty-Pownall.	8
D 19	Miss Cox.	Walter H. Pollock.	7
20	John Dennis.	Mrs. Walter H. Pollock.	6
21	Mrs. Batty.	Athol Maudslay.	5
22	A. W. Tuer.	Sir Nathaniel Staples.	4
23	Walter Ellis.	Arthur Waugh.	3
24	James Rolt.	Mrs. Brightwen.	2

Rev. Middleton Wake.

Table B (Edmund Gosse):

No.	Name	Name
13	"Times."	Helen Mat—
14	Ray Lankester, F.R.S.	G—
15	Mrs. Tweedie.	Miss Ella Cu—
16	Alexander Tweedie.	W. Earl Hol—
17	T. C. Hedderwick.	Mrs. J. K. Spe—
B 18	Mrs. H. Blackburn.	Michael Foste—
19	Henry Blackburn.	Miss Fe—
20	Mr. Kennard.	G. K. Forth—
21	Mrs. E. Kennard.	A. W. A'Bec—
22	Sir G. Douglas.	Mrs. W. Br—
23	Mrs. Gosse.	G. Du Ma—

Edmund Gosse.

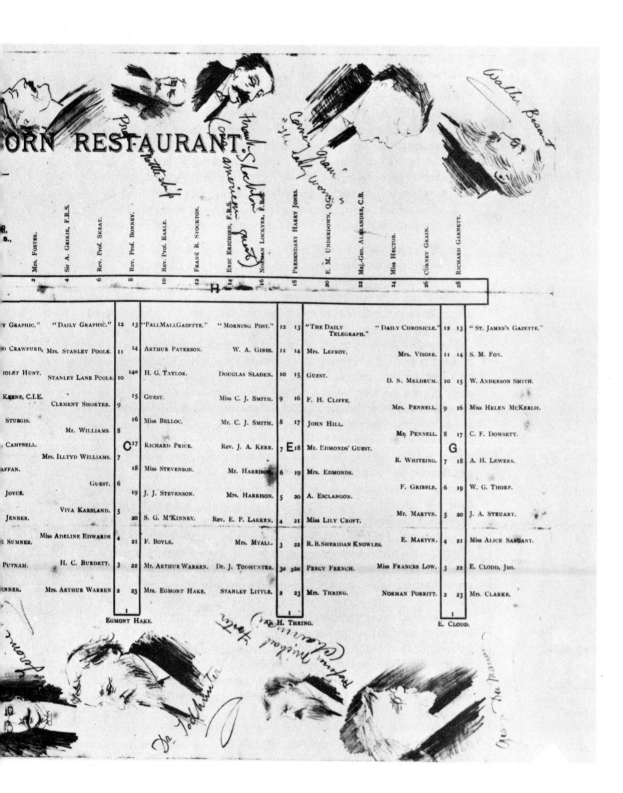

...ORN RESTAURANT.

	Mrs. Foster.	Sir A. Geikie, F.R.S.	Rev. Prof. Skeat.	Rev. Prof. Bonney.	Rev. Prof. Earle.	Frank R. Stockton.	Eric Erichsen, F.R.S.	Norman Lockyer, F.R.S.	Prebendary Harry Jones.	E. M. Underdown, Q.C.	Maj.-Gen. Alexander, C.B.	Miss Hector.	Corney Grain.	Richard Garnett.
	2	4	6	8	10	12	14	16	18	20	22	24	26	28

H

"...Y GRAPHIC."	"DAILY GRAPHIC."	12	13	"PALL MALL GAZETTE."	"MORNING POST."	12	13	"THE DAILY TELEGRAPH."	"DAILY CHRONICLE."	12	13	"ST. JAMES'S GAZETTE."
...D CRAWFURD,	Mrs. Stanley Poole,	11	14	Arthur Paterson.	W. A. Gibbs.	11	14	Mrs. Lefroy.	Mrs. Visger.	11	14	S. M. Fox.
...IOLET HUNT,	Stanley Lane Poole,	10	14a	H. G. Taylor.	Douglas Sladen.	10	15	Guest.	D. S. Meldrum.	10	15	W. Anderson Smith.
KEENE, C.I.E.	Clement Shorter,	9	15	Guest.	Miss C. J. Smith.	9	16	F. H. Cliffe.	Mrs. Pennell.	9	16	Miss Helen McKerlie.
STURGIS,	Mr. Williams,	8	16	Miss Belloc.	Mr. C. J. Smith.	8	17	John Hill.	Mr. Pennell.	8	17	C. F. Dowsett.
CAMPBELL,	Mrs. Illtyd Williams,	C	17	Richard Price.	Rev. J. A. Kerr.	E	18	Mr. Edmonds' Guest.	R. Whiteing.	G		A. H. Lewers.
...AFFAN,		7	18	Miss Stevenson.	Mr. Harrison.	6	19	Mrs. Edmonds.		7	18	
JOYCE,	Guest,	6	19	J. J. Stevenson.	Mrs. Harrison.	5	20	A. Esclangon.	F. Gribble.	6	19	W. G. Thorp.
JENNER,	Viva Karsland,	5	20	S. G. M'Kinney.	Rev. E. P. Larken.	4	21	Miss Lily Croft.	Mr. Martyn.	5	20	J. A. Steuart.
...SUMNER,	Miss Adeline Edwards,	4	21	F. Boyle.	Mrs. Myall.	3	22	R. B. Sheridan Knowles.	E. Martyn.	4	21	Miss Alice Sargant.
PUTNAM,	H. C. Burdett,	3	22	Mr. Arthur Warren.	Dr. J. Todhunter.	3a	22a	Percy French.	Miss Francks Low.	3	22	E. Clodd, Jun.
...NNER,	Mrs. Arthur Warren,	2	23	Mrs. Egmont Hake.	Stanley Little.	2	23	Mrs. Thring.	Norman Porritt.	2	23	Mrs. Clarke.
			1	Egmont Hake.			1	H. Thring.			1	E. Clodd.

19

manuscript stage.

One critic wrote of his performance:

> French's success with his audience was one of sheer personality, unaided by the elaborate training of the ordinary entertainer. In this respect he was the antithesis of a performer such as George Grossmith [an artist much admired by Percy], who had few natural gifts but who carried finish and technical polish to the highest degree. Percy French could explain very little as to how his effects were obtained; no doubt he would have benefited by academic training for the concert platform, but it would probably have injured the naturalness and spontaneity of his performance.

In 1893, again with Dr Collisson, he took a break from his touring, to successfully produce *Midsummer Madness*, a 'Music Comedietta'. This also was staged in Dublin and was the first time both appeared together on the stage in a costumed show. In one scene, the little classically-orientated Doctor appeared as 'Little Lord Faultyboy' in velvet suit and lace collar!

The touring rekindled his interest in watercolour painting, though it had never really been totally dormant. As he travelled and performed, he spent any spare time sitting alone in the most barren bogland, painting the scenery he loved best. Of the countless paintings that emanated from his brush a good 50 per cent, at least, were of that self-same apparently monotonous theme. To Percy's eye however, that scene was always different. The foreground, relieved maybe by water, gorse, heather or bog-cotton, was an admirable companion for that which attracted him most – the ever-changing skies.

In spite of his many talents, he always considered painting to be his forte. When he had collected enough pictures he would arrange exhibitions, initially in Dublin and in later years, London as well. When he had sampled the hospitality of a house on his travels, he would very often leave a picture by way of gratitude. Those aforementioned skies fascinated him so much that he would often spend his day concentrating on that aspect of his pictures, filling in the foreground that evening in his rooms.

I have read many press reports of his exhibitions and the critics were indeed profuse in their praise. In recent years his work has been fetching good prices but unfortunately this factor, and the seeming simplicity of his style, have resulted in quite a number of fakes being offered for sale. I can vouch for the reliability of that last statement as I have seen quite a number, one of which I actually purchased! So, prospective purchasers, be careful.

These artistic moorland expeditions sometimes provided an added bonus. There was for example the episode when he was sketching near Falcarragh, in the wilds of Co. Donegal, when an old women came out of a cottage with 'a cup o' tay and a bite o' griddle cake, for the dissolute

Incorporated Society of Authors.

ANNUAL DINNER,

Tuesday, 31st May, 1892.

Lord Tennyson, President.

PLAN OF TABLES.

20

stranger who was sittin' out like a shnipe in the bog.' They got into conversation as to how emigration was draining rural Ireland of her youth, leaving only the old and the very young. The old woman told him how all her boys and girls had been forced to leave for America, adding, ' 'twas a lonely land to live in when the childher was away'.

He always loved that distinctive, almost poetic turn of phrase which seems to come so naturally to the people of rural Ireland. That expression and its implications haunted him so much that he sat down in his little hotel room that night and wrote 'An Irish Mother'. I myself felt so deeply about this poem, that some years ago I set it to music. Its sincerity is for me unquestionable and moving.

An *Irish Independent* critic was to write on 27 November 1922, '. . . and the exquisite pathos of "An Irish Mother", which is a really fine poem – a poem that any writer would be proud to be father of'.

Percy French at work on a characteristic Irish landscape.

21

The musical, *Strongbow*, may have been a failure but Percy later declared it to be one of the greatest successes of his life, for he fell in love with one of the ladies who appeared in it. She was Helen Sheldon from Shipton-on-Stour, Warwickshire, then on holiday with a friend in Dublin and inveigled by her hostess to join the chorus of the show. In spite of the fact that he had remained a bachelor for so many years, Percy was missing the contentment and happiness he had found in his brief marriage. Realising he had fallen in love with Helen, who had returned to England, he courted her in a truly gallant manner, which must have left the postmen of Shipton in awe. He showered her with letters, the envelopes of which were covered front and back with the most delicate watercolours, one small 'window' being retained for the name and address.

These chivalrous attentions were successful and on 24 January 1894 they were married at Burmington Church. He brought his bride back to Ireland, and they lived initially at Mespil Road and then in Aylesbury Road, Dublin. Two daughters, Ettie and Mollie, were born in Dublin. A third daughter Joan, arrived some years later when they had moved to England. Incidentally Ettie and Joan are still fit and well and both have inherited much of their father's artistic talents and personality. The door of their quaint cottage in Suffolk is ever open and they have been unstinting in their help for a searching admirer of their illustrious father. I value their friendship highly.

During the latter years of the last century he was more and more in demand in Britain but still toured extensively throughout Ireland. He worked mainly alone but sometimes with various partners. Now and then his old friend Dr Collisson came with him and later recounted one amusing episode. He had obtained an engagement for Percy at a political assembly and on the appointed night the hall was packed to suffocation with no way through to the stage from the audience and no access at the platform end. The doctor, being responsible for the programme, was in despair as he could not find his artiste friend. Presently a leg was seen coming through a window over the platform, then a ladder was thrust through and the humorist descended it,

22

arriving amidst a bevy of MPs and their wives. It was an ideal entrance and the audience succumbed.

The French–Collisson team was a successful and ideal partnership. Though each was the direct contrast of his friend – the doctor, neat, meticulous and organised, and Percy, shabbily dressed, unpractical and bohemian – they somehow seemed to complement each other with total success. Collisson really admired Percy's talents and saw him as the 'best of men', a feeling reciprocated by his colleague. Percy was small of stature, five foot four inches in fact, but Collisson was even smaller still and, as in many a close friendship, French never let him forget the fact. He referred regularly to his friend as 'little bright eyes' and teased him endlessly over his fussiness and vain attempts to bring some organisation into Percy's life.

Collisson himself had a great sense of humour and certainly needed it on one occasion at least. When accompanying a celebrated singer of the time, Mrs Scott Fennell, at a Dublin concert, he was set to play the organ obligato to Sullivan's *The Lord Chord*, when one of the legs of his stool gave way. The audience quickly noted his predicament and when the soprano sang 'Seated one day at the organ, I was weary and ill at ease' the audience literally exploded with laughter. The embarrassed duo, with no hope of continuing, made their speedy exit.

Many years later Collisson was himself to tour Ireland with his own one-man show – but without his partner he was to meet with tepid to frigid (and in the case of Birr, blatantly hostile) receptions. In those sensitive years of Ireland's history, when a vast chasm often separated the 'gentry' from the native Irish, the latter somehow knew that Percy was laughing *with* rather than *at* them and though the doctor was proud of his Irish nationalism, as he demonstrated in his book *In and On Ireland*, he somehow was unable to convey this to his audiences. This failure hurt him deeply and after that one tour he never attempted a repeat. His itinerary took place in 1906, some five years after he had taken Holy Orders in the C. of E. and settled in a London parish.

Coincidentally the French family had also moved home that same year to London, where Percy's agent had arranged tours all over the UK. His sister however wrote in her book, 'Although my brother had his headquarters in London he was, as his wife truly says, never anything but an onlooker in London life. His heart was always with his "Dark Rosaleen" even when he was at the height of his popularity'. She loved her brother dearly and was proud of his great talents and successes, but in the same publication she strongly took him to task.

I feel that if I am to give a true picture of my brother I must not omit his faults. His habit of travelling light was a source of endless worry to his family and friends. This resulted in a most unnecessary shabbiness of appearance which lost him many good engagements. He would not pay the slightest attention to business which he was perfectly capable to transacting, if he would only do so. His greatest fault was his disregard for his own and his family's prosperity.

He just did not seem to realise the importance of such details.

Letter from Percy French to his daughter Ettie.

24

The result of his increasing homesickness was that his Irish tours became a regular annual practice until the end of his career. So, for several months every year he would vanish from the London scene to seek his essential antidote in the village halls and countryside of his beloved Ireland.

Appearing in a concert at London's Steinway Hall, shortly after his arrival, he was approached by two leading agents, George Ashton and Gerald Christie, who had been very moved and impressed by his act. This meeting resulted in many excellent engagements, the most prestigious, possibly, being an invitation to appear before the Prince of Wales, later King Edward VII. This royal seal of aproval, added to the personal letter of thanks and appreciation he received from His Highness, and the consequent invitations to return, obviously helped his career considerably.

It seems he became very popular with the entire Royal Family, and was commissioned by them personally to paint several pictures – two especially requested as wedding presents for the Queen of Spain. For over a decade he held annual exhibitions of his watercolours at the Modern Gallery, Bond Street. Shortly after one of his appearances at Sandringham, the Queen and Princess Mary visited another Bond Street gallery, where a couple of Percy's works were inconspicuously displayed. The Princess suddenly stopped before them and said, 'Oh! Mother, here are some of Mr French's pictures! you know he draws upside down?' He was the only artist she bothered to comment on. The Royal children had obviously given him their own special seal of approval.

He was neither overawed nor overimpressed by these voyages into society. Once he was engaged to make an after-dinner appearance at the London home of a well-known aristocratic family. Arriving at the agreed time, he was told to wait in the hall until his services were required. He waited for some considerable time and then made his way down to the domestic quarters where before long he had a party in full swing. Eventually, the elite upstairs deigned to send word that they were now ready to be entertained. The message they received in return was

25

Percy French

that 'Mr French presents his compliments but regretted that he had already given his performance in the kitchens'. The fact that he lost the substantial fee involved was of secondary importance. He was often heard to compliment an audience, made up of the cream of society, on their intelligent comprehension of his wit.

Even his Royal associations left him unmoved. He recorded his feelings on the subject:

> As an entertainer I have met Kings and Queens and blue-blooded potentates of all shapes and sizes, but as their remarks consisted of 'thank you *so* much, Mr French, we *have* enjoyed ourselves'. Or 'Really! Mr French, that last sketch was just too, TOO clever', I don't think these polite platitudes are worth recording.
>
> Now, if the late Queen Victoria had buttonholed me as I was packing up my chalks and asked me; 'Why should Russia not have Constantinople?', the Battle of Plevna might never have been fought! Or if King Edward had suggested a 'bottle of bubbly and a Woodbine in my little den', and told me how his mother had persistently thwarted his lifelong wish to be a comedian, I could make up a most interesting chapter of social tittle-tattle.

26

But these great people do not consult me about the balance of power or the choice of a career, so I devote my writing to the people I have met and really conversed with .

One letter from the Prince of Wales, from Sandringham, thanks him for his gift of the book of watercolours and the 'plate'. These 'plates' were a speciality of his, bestowed on special friends. He would hold a plate over a candle until it was blackened by the flame. Then he could work out the most exquisite pictures as he erased sections of the smoked surface with the wrong end of his brush. Since they were obviously so fragile, few have survived.

Other by-products of his work that have not survived were the thousands of chalk drawings which he liberally turned out during his stage act. I found the answer to this scarcity myself when appearing with a similar act just a few years ago. My young son, who was standing in the wings with me, was enthralled by the cleverness of the 'trick drawings' and after the show he asked the artist if he would let him have one of the drawings as a souvenir. 'Not on your life', was the reply, 'I don't want you finding out how I do it and then pinching my act'.

Jack McKenna from Armagh has sent me the following very revealing anecdote:

While a schoolboy I went into the City Hall in Armagh where Mr French had given a concert the previous night. He was tearing up the pictures he had drawn the night before during his show. I helped him and when we had them all torn up, we burned them in the City Hall yard. I have regretted it ever since that I did not ask him for one of them.

He mentioned in the course of our conversation that there had been a good house for his show. He asked me the price of admission and I told him it was one shilling, two shillings and three shillings. Very young though I was, it struck me that he was not a business-man for he told me that, 'the prices were a robbery for listening and watching an old man amusing himself'.

His wife Helen had really got to work in bringing some organisation into his otherwise disordered life. Having settled at 48 Springfield Road, North West London – between Kilburn and Maida Vale – she insisted on keeping a personal diary of all his engagements, with the fees meticulously noted to each. To that part of his life and to his life while under the family roof she could lovingly bring some order, but once away from that tender haven, he would always and ever be the impracticable bohemian, unmindful of regularity, order or appearance. That was something nobody could ever change. Though he had a remarkable physical resemblance to Mark Twain, he was utterly unique in every other aspect.

His Steinway Hall concerts became annual events for which he used a variety of accompanists and partners, but inevitably he and Dr Collisson teamed up together again for one of these and were a tremendous success. I note at the end of one of the programmes that 'All Doctor Collisson's fees etc. are given away in Charity'! The reunion also produced the successful *Noah's Ark*, a Christmas fantasy for children, presented at the Waldorf in 1906. One reviewer called it, 'a piece of great charm and originality'. The doctor also accompanied him on some of his provincial dates.

In one letter to his wife from Newquay in Cornwall Percy wrote,

> My life consists of eating large meals and painting two pictures daily which we auction. The Cornish Coast doesn't appeal to me, being mostly precipitous cliffs and tiny bays. The good old sun bursting over the bog is what I love most. Rudyard Kipling was in the audience last night.

By 1908 he was also exhibiting at the New Dudley Gallery in Piccadilly and the Modern Gallery, Bond Street, while appearing at the St George's Hall in a show, with the famous 'Maskelyne and Devant'. Songs were flowing from his pen and being published, with 'McBreen's Heifer', 'Whistlin' Phil McHugh', 'Eileen Og', 'Darlin' Girl from Clare', 'Donnegan's Daughter', and 'Fr O'Callaghan', being about the best known. Two others deserve special mention since their source of

28

inspiration is interesting.

In Co. Clare ran the little narrow gauge railway line, 'The West Clare Railway', which went from Ennis to Kilkee and was used regularly by Percy, as he loved that part of Ireland very much. Since a veritable folklore has grown up around this now famous railway, and fact and fiction are becoming increasingly difficult to unravel, I will endeavour to be as factual as possible. People have verified that they have often sat in their carriage, the train halted in the wilds of the Clare countryside, and watched the driver dismount from his engine and meander across a field to deliver a parcel to some lonely cottager. Judging by the length of time spent inside the house, these eye-witnesses maintained he had time, at least, for some refreshments! The train was seen many a time, having already moved out of the station, to stop and reverse back again, as some late arrival had appeared on the platform. Others have told me of getting onto the train in the icy depths of winter and being presented with metal containers, filled with boiling water, to keep their feet warm.

There was a certain Michael Talty, employed by the company for many years, who it seems was the inspiration for Percy's song 'Are Ye Right There Michael'. Typical of the stories told to me by locals, with hand innocently on heart and fingers crossed, is this one. It seems that the train was 'speeding' through the countryside one day when it suddenly and very abruptly pulled up, miles from civilisation. Someone poked their head out of a window and yelled, 'What's wrong, Michael?'. 'Ah!, there's an ould cow on the line', came the reply. Eventually the train moved off and for over half an hour happily puffed its way through the countryside. Suddenly it came to a halt once again. 'What's wrong Michael,' yelled the same passenger. 'Is there another cow on the line?' 'No,' says the redoubtable Michael, 'It's the same one!'

Fact or fiction, it certainly was no 'Flying Scotsman', and on one occasion at least Percy arrived on it late for a concert in Kilkee. So late, in fact, that the disappointed audience had already had their money refunded. Herewith is an excerpt from a Digest of Court cases of the 1890s, applicable to various Irish Railway Companies. This paragraph of indisputable authenticity reads:

Railway – *Passenger.*

1. — **Delay** — *Breakdown*] Where plaintiff claimed £10 as damages owing to his having missed a concert by reason of a breakdown on the defendant company's line:- *Held*, the company were liable for damages in the amount claimed. *French* v. *West Clare Railway Company*

Co.Ct..31 I. L. T,140

Some have written describing a burlesqued court scene, wherein Percy was sued by the Railway Company for either slander or libel. I can find no evidence of this.

29

Thomas Mason of Dublin, who had toured with him, wrote:

Percy French's well-known song about the West Clare Railway is really an excellent description of the working of that remarkable line, at least in those days. Once when travelling on it during very hot weather, the whole train was held up at a wayside station while the station master procured glasses of water for Mr French and myself from his well, pumping away quite unconcernedly for a couple of minutes.

He goes on to verify the late arrival in Kilkee and the reimbursement of the audience, continuing, 'Mr French took an action against the company for damages. It so happened that the judge who tried the case had a similar experience and so had a fellow feeling with Mr French who triumphantly won'.

On our tours he usually went out sketching in the mornings. I helped him to prepare lantern slides; in getting the halls ready for his entertainment and in collecting the money at the door. One of our chief difficulties was to procure footlights, about which, and lighting in general, Mr French was very particular. I often had to commandeer footlights in the shape of kitchen oil lamps from all the local shops and even from private houses.

But travelling with him was by no means all lilies and roses! On arriving in Larne, where he had expected a very good audience, he decided to send the money received elsewhere home to his family at once, as he disliked travelling with large sums about him. Unfortunately the house did not materialise and we were left with so little in hand that we had to take *very* third-rate lodgings. It was very amusing to hear Mr French dodging the questions of his friends as to where he was staying and trying to prevent them from calling to see him at his 'Hotel'!

Back to his compositions, and perhaps his most famous of all, 'The Mountains of Mourne'. He describes its birth:

Looking at the range of the Mourne Mountains from Skerries [on the east coast and some 20 miles north of Dublin] one clear afternoon, I found myself repeating 'The Mountains of Mourne sweep down to the sea'. This line kept recurring to me till one day it wedded itself to an old Irish air, and the combination seemed so happy that I set to work, or rather shut myself up in my top room with pen, ink and paper, and waited. And so my most successful song, admirably arranged by Doctor Collisson, was given to an applauding public.

Now a major part of my attraction for and devotion to Percy French, has been greatly influenced by the fact that so many of his poems and compositions were credible because they were the products of real events and associations. So, when Messrs Pigott, who were his prime publishers, allowed me to see the original manuscript, I noted the address at the top. It read '27, Clifton Hill London N.W.'. The family had by then adventurously moved to a house round the corner.

Knowing how he had so often used his characters to express his own feelings, I realised, on noting that address, that the Irish lad, alone and lonely in London, was really Percy himself, missing his beloved homeland and friends and characteristically successfully treading that thin borderline twixt humour and sadness. He had observed at an early age the close kinship of tears and laughter.

'Are Ye Right There, Michael?':
cartoon by Rowel Friers.

By April 1910, we find him appearing utterly 'solo', at Dublin's famed Abbey Theatre and being given front page prominence in *The Irish Society and Social Review*.

> We do not often see him in Dublin now-a-days. Mr French's versatility, and his varied interests and occupations bring him into touch with most of the artistic activities in London, theatrical, journalistic and literary. He is a well-known figure on big nights at the Savage Club, the Green Room or the Press Club. But he still remains as Bohemian as we have always known him, and the long elaborate dinners with which London always celebrates great occasions, and to which he is constantly being invited are to him inflictions to be escaped whenever possible.

That reference to his 'bohemian' trait is interesting in that he was a founder member of the 'Bohemians' – a group of Dublin musical enthusiasts who congregated weekly, and still do to this day, at a city hotel and either entertain each other or invite guests to contribute. My own first vocal efforts before a Dublin public were in fact for the same 'Bohs'. I was already being privately trained there under the kind and able patronage of Dr Vincent O'Brien and his famed one-time pupil Count John McCormack. As I sang my classical and operatic selection, standing beneath a huge oil painting of Percy French, I little realised how our lives would one day become so closely intertwined, albeit posthumously.

By 1910 the stars of French and Collisson were really in the ascendant, and they were offered a tour of Canada, the USA and the West Indies. In late September they were given an elaborate send-off by the Savage Club, the occasion immortalised by an excellent caricatured poster. At Paddington Station, boy scouts, waifs and strays, artists and musicians (including two Irish pipers complete in saffron kilts) united to speed the travellers. Once on board ship they soon realised that the majority of their fellow voyagers were young Irish boys and girls on their way to the New World, forced to emigrate, as so many of their forebears had, from their much loved, but troubled and poverty-

32

stricken motherland.

In this day and age of supersonic flight and interplanetary travel, it is difficult to conceive what emigration meant in those times. Very often, whenever some young member of a family was forced to sail on the 'emigrant ship' the clan would get together and hold an 'American Wake'. The atmosphere was almost that of a funeral wake, for the distance involved meant that there was, in their minds, an equal chance of ever seeing their loved one again. It was indeed an occasion for lament and sadness.

It was in that company and atmosphere that French and Collisson found themselves on board this transatlantic steamer. Percy recorded an incident which occurred as the passengers stood at the rail sadly watching the coast of Ireland gradually receding into the distance. Beside him stood two young lads and as they watched, one remarked to the other, 'Ye know Mick, they'll be cuttin' the corn in Creeshlough the day'. The poignancy of this remark and all its implications stirred him so much that he sat down and tried to visualise the thoughts and feelings of that lad, who was probably leaving for ever everything he loved, his family, friends and girl friend and his beloved Donegal village of Creeshlough. It has been written, 'Laughing, the Irishman mourns', and betwixt a smile and a tear Percy wrote that imaginary missive to the friend still living at home. 'The Emigrant's Letter' was introduced to an enthusiastic audience on 7 October at their first concert in the Winsor Hall, Montreal.

Their versatile and cultured breath of Ireland was avidly devoured by homesick fellow countrymen. These were the same Irish emigrants who some years later were to carry the young John McCormack into that realm of superstar where he might never otherwise have dwelt. For these talented artists were to give their brothers-in-exile an identity, and prove to the numerous other nationalities in the American melting-pot, that Ireland could contribute talent and culture as well as emigrés. Incredibly, today, though the works of Shaw, Wilde, Goldsmith, Swift, Yeats, Joyce and innumerable others have been read and respected throughout the entire world, many are still apparently unconvinced.

The Canadian press were generous in their praise, with such quotes as 'a brilliant success – French's delivery is delicious', 'The whole programme is delivered with an aplomb, a finish, a studied artistry devoid of any suggestion of laboured sketch, and introduces one to the real thing'. Ettie and Joan French have many times mentioned to me that, 'the nearest contemporary counterpart of the French/Collisson duo would be the Flanders/Swann partnership', though the latter, while brilliant, had nothing like the versatility of the originals.

From Canada they came to New York, where their agent, J.C. Duff, had booked them into Daly's Theatre and the Mendelssohn Hall, followed by Albany, Cincinnati etc. Everywhere they were acclaimed:

. . . the folks laughed till they were tired and their sides hurt . . .

French and Collisson are Irishmen, cultured and clever: how the astute vaudeville magnates of this country have allowed this pair to remain unmolested is a mystery. In a 45 or 50 minute act they could be worth $2,500 a week to any circuit in the country.

These gentlemen are artists in their line, as great as the famous stars are in theirs.

Percy's resemblance to Mark Twain was often commented upon.

Busy though he was, he always seemed to find the time to write lengthy letters to his wife and daughters. Those to his wife were a veritable diary of events with humorous glimpses into his relationship with Doctor Collisson. Though ever respectful and fond of each other these two never overstepped the threshold of familiarity, always addressing each other as 'French' and 'Collisson'. The letters and poems to Ettie, Molly and Joan were loving and tenderly paternal and painstakingly composed in a style that would appeal to their respective ages. Though careless of many things he was ever and always most solicitous in writing to his family whilst touring. His earlier 'picture' letters and rhymes to the younger daughters were quite original, using pictures instead of words e.g. a 'deer' for dear etc.

Their agent arranged for their engagements in the West Indies, where a smallpox scare put them, with their fellow tourists, in quarantine. Ever resourceful, Percy used his spare time to capture the Caribbean landscapes in watercolour. The sense of values of the Bermudians and their barter system was just what appealed to Percy's outlook. In one letter to his family, signed 'Wandering William' he wrote 'no money ever seems to change hands and yet no bill is ever sent at all. A man died here lately who owed 30 years subscription to the local newspaper. His heirs hadn't any money to pay up with, so they did a fair thing — they renewed the subscription!!!!!' The engagements eventually fulfilled, they resumed their homeward voyage.

Letter from Percy French to his daughter Ettie.

34

HOTEL WESTMINSTER
BOSTON, MASSACHUSETTS
C. A. GLEASON

To Ette (nov. 4. 1910)

I've wandered round Toronto
I've wandered round Quebec
Yet can't find what I want to
See hanging round your neck

2

I saw some pretty trinkets
Some jewels that might do
But always said "I think its
not good enough for you".

3

I've searched in Boston city
I've searched in Montreal
And the burden of my ditty
Is — there's nothing there at all

4

Its really most distressing
my search has been in vain
So I'm sending you my blessing
and these fancies from my brain

J00LER.

5

They will fly across the water
To the home in Clifton Hill
and tell my dear dear
daughter
That I'm thinking of
her still.

35

Percy's 'one-time' boss and 'all-time' confidante, R.J. Mecredy later wrote, 'Percy French on one occasion made a lengthy visit to America and returned with a well filled purse as a reward for his labours. Unfortunately, however, the person to whom he entrusted the investment of the money on his return to London, defaulted. French took the matter in his usual philosophic spirit'. So it was just as well that their agent, J.C. Duff, had enterprisingly published a brochure in London, with quotes from their tour critiques. What promoters could resist such quotes as:

'Few funnier things have been heard in New York in a long time.' – N.Y. *Tribune*

'The audience simply roared, Laugh? There was nothing else to do.' – N.Y. *World*

These, added to the quotes already mentioned, provided formidable publicity.

The engagements flowed in and late in 1913 Percy chose to accept some engagements in Switzerland. He had always expressed his feelings that this was the only country besides Ireland he really wanted to paint and this doubtlessly influenced his decision to go. Again lengthy letters, mainly to 'dear Mummy', flowed back to the home at Clifton Hill. While these gave but passing references to his professional pursuits, he filled pages with his observations of life on the ski slopes. Many of his appearances there were for the 'waifs and strays', a charity near and dear to his friend Dr Collisson, now back tending his London parochial flock.

He returned to London and a full diary. Songs, verse and prose still emanated from the talented mind and gems such as 'The Hoodoo', 'Mrs Brady', 'The Oklahoma Rose', and 'Sweet Marie' were instant successes. Cocking a snook at the superficial and often contrived pathos of the prevalent music-hall song, he wrote 'That's why we're buryin' him'. His talented eldest daughter Ettie set it to music most efficiently and effectively, as did her younger sister Molly, some forty years later, with several other lyrics, such as 'Ach, I dunno!', 'Little Bridget Flynn',

Percy French.

37

and 'Ballymilligan'.

Some time prior to this, while re-visiting his beloved Cavan, he learned that his one-time jaunting-car 'chauffeur' and friend, Paddy Reilly, had emigrated. For all time Paddy will be remembered in Percy's haunting 'Come Back Paddy Reilly to Ballyjamesduff'.

While 1914 saw him back in London on the threshold of even greater fame, it also abruptly brought his hopes and dreams, and that of much of humanity, to a deafening disintegration, with the outbreak of World War I.

Suddenly, the gentle little inoffensive artist and entertainer was a complete misfit in the new, noisy, strident, marching atmosphere. He had never been able to generate in himself the slightest interest in politics, let alone war, seemingly only being able to view such harsh realities through his historical satires and comic war escapades, such as 'Slattery's Mounted Fut' and 'Andy McElroe'. Only his deep love of 'Dark Rosaleen' had inspired such historic and patriotic lines as his 'Galloping Hogan' and 'When Erin Wakes'.

He did write and publish several war songs like 'Am Tag' and 'All by the Baltic Say', but his heart was simply not in it. Entertainers were offering their services to entertain troops and this he readily did both in Britain and on the Continent. Schools and colleges, ever eager to welcome his inimitable act, saw more and more of him, and I have had many letters from ex-pupils, who though now in the twilight of their years, still retain vivid memories of 'Mr Percy French' and his annual visits – surely a special tribute in itself.

For his public engagements he enrolled the services of an assistant. Florence Marks filled the bill for some time only to be followed by the talented May Laffan. His *Dublin Up To Date* show had been such a great success some twenty-five years before that he updated the contents and once again drew full houses to the Little Theatre, Sackville (now O'Connell) St, Dublin. As with all his work during these years, a generous percentage was always donated to the Red Cross. A backer offered to stage the show in London and just as everything seemed poised for success the Irish 'Easter Rising' took place and no Irish entertainment had the remotest hope of success on that side of the water.

A deep, deep sadness at the troubles his beloved Ireland was undergoing, coupled with setbacks in his health, had taken much of the spring from his step. The family had noted his failing health and did everything humanly possible to persuade him to be less demanding on himself and periodically rest. Their efforts were utterly fruitless. Still in 1916, as he was setting off for a concert in Bray from Blackrock Station, the train began to move from the platform. He attempted to jump on the moving train, missed and lost his footing, only to be dragged along the platform for some distance until the train could be stopped. He was badly bruised and shaken.

Opposite: Percy French, the indefatigable traveller.

38

Friends who saw him after this episode were shocked by the deterioration in his health and most believe his decline started with that accident. Stubbornly, he still carried on as though he were still the fit tennis-playing, marathon-cycling lad of the 1880s. Nor was his irrepressible outlook dimmed. While a very bad air-raid shook North London, he sat with his family and some neighbours in a 'garden room' at their home. Keeping them entertained with relaxing chatter for the duration of the raid, he remarked, when the 'all-clear' eventually sounded, 'Do you know, I think that was quite the pleasantest raid we have had!'

The war ended and he continued the same pattern of life. As late as 1916 he was undertaking incredible itineraries. When my friend, BBC producer Alan Tongue, and I were preparing some TV shows on the great man, Ettie and Joan French kindly gave us access to his diaries. We were astounded! Alan had a map of Ireland on the wall of his office with a red dot marking every concert venue mentioned in those diaries. In spite of the fact that these must have represented but a fraction of those visited and re-visited many times over during his entire career, the effect was that of a large dog whose entire body was covered by measles. No city, town, village or parish was left unvisited. He somehow managed to wend his tortuous way through some 27 venues in a month of 31 days, jumping from Portstewart to Bray, thence to Cork, Lahinch and the south-west; suddenly appearing in Ballycastle and the north-west followed by Bundoran and ending the month back in Co. Wicklow. From there it was usually back to Britain and more work.

In January 1920 he accepted a Scottish tour, in spite of the efforts of his worried wife and daughters to convince him of the wisdom of giving up winter touring at least and devoting that time to relaxed painting and restful London engagements. Before his show at the Palette Club in Glasgow his assistant May Laffan noted how very ill he looked. Her efforts to dissuade him from appearing were in vain and with typical iron will he completed the strenuous show.

As May was seeing him off for Liverpool the next morning he promised the anxious girl that he would stop at the home of his cousin in Formby and take a good rest. As he bade her good-bye he thanked her, rather significantly, for having 'played the game to the end'!

When he eventually arrived, his cousin Canon Richardson at once realised he was seriously ill and the doctor was called in. Pneumonia was diagnosed and Mrs French was wired for and duly arrived. Just when he seemed to be recovering his heart failed and on Saturday, 24 January 1920, still only sixty-six, he died. He was buried the following Tuesday in the beautifully peaceful St Luke's graveyard, where, to this very day, nothing seems to have altered.

His old friend Dr Collisson was shattered by the news and held a memorial service for his much-loved friend in his London church. Incredibly, he himself was dead before that week was out.

40

Likewise, all those for whom Percy French had been a living legend were heartbroken, for I have found ample evidence that few, if any, have inspired such love and respect as he, with never a hint of the contrary. Though a Protestant of the landlord gentry class, prayers were said for him in Roman Catholic churches throughout Ireland, while in the Sacred Heart Church of the same faith in Quex Road, Kilburn, London (his parish, and coincidentally the first I visited and settled in when I came to England), Masses were held for the repose of his soul.

Percy French with his second wife Helen.

41

Tributes filled the Press. The public just could not comprehend that this institution, this talented Peter Pan, was no more. His sister Emily Lucy (Mrs DeBurgh Daly) published her *Chronicles and Poems of Percy French* in 1922 and I am much in debt to that volume for various pieces of first-hand information. Strangely, many years later, it was her daughter, Lucy Daly, who was to collect me in her car at Dublin Airport and drive me to Cloonyquin House, then still standing, for the Percy French Festival, where I also met Ettie and Joan for the first time.

One feature of the *Chronicles* was an eloquent 'foreword' written by the eminent Irish author Katharine Tynan. Percy had been a frequent visitor to the Tynan home near Claremorris, usually arriving early in the day carrying only a paint-box, palette and sketching board and having already forgotten at which shop near Claremorris Station he had left his luggage. In this sensitively written piece Katharine Tynan seemed to sum up all the sentiments felt by those who had really known this 'Last of the Troubadours'.

> Percy French was so versatile, so quick witted, so extraordinarily accomplished in such a variety of ways, so sensitive to human and natural appeals that one must think of him as having a touch of that quality by which talent is dull – the quality of genius. The general public knew him as an Irish entertainer, whose entertainments were purely human in fantasy, with sensitive touches of pathos – entertainments from which one came happy and uplifted. He loved the innocent love-making, the innocent domesticities. He was incapable of vulgarity and he had a unique gift of making his audiences love him.
>
> He was thoroughly amiable and benevolent. One thinks of him as incapable of harshness or unkindness or of dishonour or meanness. He had a unique sense of the oddities and whimsicalities of his country people.
>
> His watercolours of Ireland, flung out with a lavish prodigality, bestowed upon friends or sold for a song, are, now that the incessantly working hand is stilled, coming into their own. He is the interpreter of still life, land and skyscape in Western Ireland.

42

He grew up to the bogs and the mountains and the great skies and the atmosphere, clear as crystal, of Western Ireland. He let the country make its own appeal, express its own significance. The cottages ('nearly always!') make the only human touch in his pictures.

Let us touch on the man himself. He was most lovable and impossibly unpractical. The Good Fairy who rained so many gifts into his cradle had forgotten or disdained the drab but useful gift of being practical. He was more unpractical than anyone I have ever known. Fortunately he usually found a friend willing to undertake the practical side of things for him, though the result was occasionally despairing, when he chose to intervene, which happily was not often. Once, when I had been selling pictures for him, he arrived on the scene and gave a much larger choice at a quarter of the price. He was incapable of bartering. To give would have been his choice. He had nothing at all to do with the money-changers who were driven out of the temple.

The hard realities of life must have forced themselves upon him several times, but he fortified himself against them, wrapping himself in a cloak of dreams. One often wondered what happened when he went on tour, say in England. Ireland was studded up and down with people who loved him and laughed while they undertook his business.

He had great sorrow in his life and like many artists he had seen men acclaimed who were mere journeymen in his profession and could be nothing else. But he was never soured. The things that might have soured other natures but sweetened his. There was much of the immortal child about him to the end. He never wearied of his art and he was unceasingly industrious at it even when his bodily health was failing.

A fine, brave, clean gentleman, loving his kind, without guile, simple and honourable. That was Percy French as seen by his friends and lovers.

The Irish Times remembered him thus:

He contributed much to the joy of life and wherever he went he shed about him an atmosphere of goodwill. He possessed rare gifts of art and humour – an art apparently slight and effortless, yet beautiful and by no means superficial in its simplicity; a humour free from burlesque, which never consciously hurt the most sensitive soul. Percy French's nature was as simple as a child's. He was never happier than while he was having a romp with the little ones, and the grown-ups were to him only bigger children waiting to be amused. The first impression one had of W.P.F. was the sadness of his face. Apart from one great sorrow his life was not an unhappy one, but he loved his Dark Rosaleen and something of her sadness was always with him.

My friend, Alan Tongue, during his research for our programmes on Percy French visited Glenveigh Castle in Co. Donegal where the wandering entertainer had been a regular guest. Alan found that on one visit he had written the following epitaph, premature yet typical, into the visitors' book:

Remember me is all I ask and yet
If the remembrance prove a task – forget!

Portrait of Percy French by
Robert Ponsonby Staples
(*Collection, Ulster Museum, Belfast*)

I believe Percy French decided on the location of several of his songs merely because their melodic sounding names suited his purpose. Places like Petravore, Drumcolliher, Inishmeela, Ballybay etc., rolled easily off the tongue. Little did he realise when he wrote 'Donnegan's Daughter', and had Donnegan himself returning from 'The States' to his home in Ballyporeen, that that same village would in 1981 make world headlines as the descendant of another of its sons became President of the United States – President Ronald Reagan.

It seems inevitable that the work of Percy French (whose whole life was devoted to living among, observing and writing about, that which he loved most in life, Ireland and her people) should gradually be absorbed into our folklore. Already tales are told of his exploits and the sources from whence he found the inspiration for many of his songs. Mostly these bear no relation to fact but I avidly collect each anecdote, as so often they are gems of Irish humour and imagination.

The tales told about the West Clare Railway would alone take hours to recount. During my lecture on Percy French at the Royal Dublin Society some years ago I mentioned this fact to my audience, adding that though I knew people were 'having me on' very often, I really relished the stories.

Into my dressing-room, after my lecture, came a tall, elegant, stern-visaged Church of Ireland clergyman, possibly in his early eighties. He introduced himself and continued, 'I heard what you said, but I am a clergyman and wouldn't lie to you'!!!?

He proceeded to tell me how, as a boy in his native Lahinch, he found himself one day sitting in a carriage of the West Clare train, which already had been standing at the platform for some half an hour after its scheduled departure time. Seeing no apparent cause for the delay he enquired the reason from another young lad. 'The guard can't start the train,' came the reply, 'because his whistle's broken'.

My narrator joined the band on the platform and asked the guard himself to elucidate. 'Look,' says the man, 'can't you see, I've lost the pea out of me whistle!'

Suggested remedies poured in. 'Why not wave a flag or a handkerchief' sounding the most constructive.

'Oh begob no!' says the guard. 'You see, I am issued with a list of regulations by the head-office and it says there distinctly, that "every train has to be started by the blast of a whistle".'

It was stalemate till somebody proposed, 'Why not give this young lad a shillin' and send him up to the shop for a bag of peas'. All agreed that this was indeed sound wisdom.

Off ran the lad and some 20 minutes later returned breathless with the salvation of the situation. The guard opened the bag and peered inside. They were split peas! 'These are no use to me,' says he.

'For God's sake,' shouted an irate passenger, 'will you put one in and make a peep of some description.'

My ecclesiastical informant looked at me, sincerity shining from his benevolent eyes, and continued, 'And do you know, Mr O'Dowda, he put one in and blew the whistle, but only half the train pulled out! Luckily my brother Frank was with me that evening and can always bear testimony to my veracity.'

The factual anecdotes of his one-time touring managers and partners, Messrs Franklin and Mason, were often better than the fictional. The former remembered that formidable human obstacle to successful touring, namely the provincial bill-poster. Seemingly Percy would vanish when it came to settling the bill and Franklin, who doubled as a violinist-cum-manager, had to query the absence of any posters in the vicinity, though some fifty had been sent in advance. The excuse given was the universal one. 'Sure the wind and the rain have given them a terrible beltin' on the hoardin's and walls and destroyed them.' I can personally vouch for the credibility of such a scene, for on my own tours I have seen my bills making their first appearance the day following my visit and have had first-hand accounts of fellow artistes finding bundles of unused posters and handbills hidden at the rear of some remote pub.

Franklin also remembers one trip from Kilrush via the Tarbert Ferry to Ballybunion. He had wired for transport to meet them at the ferry. Sure enough it was there – a lanky lad driving a straggling horse which, it turned out, had been working on the farm since dawn. After the poor beast had made countless stops for a rest, the compassionate pair decided to walk, carrying their own bags and instruments. Eventually an old farmer driving a load of turf took pity on them and they made a unique entrance into Ballybunion with the farmer leading the way carrying a lantern, followed by the turf cart bearing the baggage on its crest and the tired travellers completing the quaint procession at the rear.

The monorail from Ballybunion to Listowel somehow escaped the satirised fate of the West Clare, though Percy had often travelled on it. It was an ingenious invention with only one rail and the compartments on either side, precariously near the ground. For all the world it looked like two creels of turf on either side of a donkey. Once when French and

46

Franklin were travelling on it, the guard approached them and whispered 'Would you ever mind crossing to the other side Surs and help to balance the weight of the other passengers.'

Percy never intentionally offended anyone but one song of his certainly gave him an embarrassing experience. With a full house and an enthusiastic audience at a country hall, he began to sing one of his current favourites – 'The Night That Miss Cooney Eloped' – with a local sweep, incidentally! As he sang, the audience at the rear and middle of the hall first began to titter and then uncontrollably laugh till the entire hall seemed convulsed. That is, all except the occupants of the first two rows – a solid mass of prosperous people who sat like graven images, not a smile on their faces. They endured the song for about two verses and then made a formidable marching exit.

It turned out that they were all members of the Cooney family and Miss Cooney, the daughter of the principal trader in the area, had actually eloped the previous night. Though Percy was totally ignorant of all this, most people believed he had either written or performed it specially for the occasion.

Once he was in conversation with a West of Ireland farmer who had just returned from a visit to 'The Meeting of the Waters' at Avoca, that exquisite spot that had inspired the pen of Thomas Moore. Percy asked the old boy what he thought of it. 'Is it what did I think of it ye ask, Mr French?' says he. 'Well now, to be candid wid ye Sir, I didn't think much of it, at all. For all I seen was two small sthrames an' forty acres of the worst land in Ireland.'

I was reminded of this typically rural Irish, down-to-earth attitude some years ago when I was standing looking on the majestic grandeur of the Dingle peninsula. It was a calm summer evening with a red sun sinking into a placid Atlantic ocean. I was unashamedly near to tears as I beheld the beauty of it all. To complete the picture an old man slowly approached me driving a solitary cow. He bade me the time of day and I replied, 'Isn't it really beautiful here?' Without even raising his head he retorted, 'Begob then! you should try livin' in it.' Not until I noted the trees and hedges bent to a 45 degrees angle by the raging storms and the houses with their westerly facing windows bricked up in defence of the raging Atlantic, did I realise the legitimacy of his challenge.

In her fine book, *The Careys*, Honor Rudnitzky tells of Percy French's visits to the home of that talented Ulster family, whose paternal head, Joseph, was an artist of considerable talent. She tells of his involvement with their Sketching Club, which was also patronised by one of Ireland's finest and most original artists, William Conor. His affection for children was also noted, but seemingly having Percy as a house guest had one drawback, for Mrs Carey confided to the author's mother 'you know he's just wiped his brushes on the new spare-room wallpaper'.

Some years ago I was appearing on the Ed Sullivan show on CBS Television – networked throughout the USA and Canada. The producer had especially asked me to include 'McBreen's Heifer', with Ed asking me to explain the 'match-making' system. Afterwards I had a letter from a gentleman saying that he was writing on behalf of an organisation with a membership of many thousands of Montana cattlemen. He requested that I send him the words and music of that song as they would like to 'adopt it as their anthem, to be sung at all future meetings, conventions and banquets'. I did as he requested, but I have never found out if the 'cattlemen's anthem' was ever actually performed. If it had been, then I am sure that Percy, in his heavenly haven, must have viewed the scene with great delight, as the multitude of muscular Montana cattlemen stood to attention, stone-faced and serious, and sung his ingenious ditty. Come to think of it maybe he has got the cherubim, seraphim and thrones doing precisely the same up there.

A few final personal thoughts – people have expressed to me the opinion that their personal criticism of Percy French's style was based on their opinion that it was too simple. It is that very aspect I consider to be the secret of his success. Since he usually wrote of the loves, laments and laughter of the ordinary folk, he obviously intentionally used simple basic language, never employing a lengthy or uncommon word where a more ordinary one would suffice. His writing could be understood by all. He had shown in his editorial days with *The Jarvey* that he could flex his muscles of verbosity when he wished. While those efforts have been all but forgotten his 'simple'! prose, poems, plays, parodies and paintings will surely be remembered as long as there is an Ireland.

He was born in 1854 into a land struggling to recover from the horrible devastation wrecked by that famine of the 1840s which had either killed or scattered several millions of Ireland's population. His family had always treated their staff and tenants extremely well, even maintaining a school on the estate specially for the children. So, not unexpectedly, the French family suffered badly economically, till eventually they too had lost everything.

When I first visited Cloonyquin in the 1950s I was most impressed by the obvious love and respect that endured for the French family among the people of that area. Percy French they knew full well was one of them and understood, loved and respected them. While he could observe the humour of certain aspects of their lives, he also genuinely suffered with them in their adversities. Till the day he died his heart was ever with his 'Dark Rosaleen' and her family, of which he was indisputably one.

I was born a boy and have remained
one ever since

William Percy French 1854-1920

48

SONGS

PERCY FRENCH

Abdallah Bulbul Ameer

Words and music by
PERCY FRENCH

1. Oh the sons of the pro-phet are har-dy and grim, and quite un-ac-cus-tom'd to fear — But none were so reck-less of life or of limb, as Ab-dal-lah Bul-bul A-meer — When they want-ed a man to en-cour-age the van, or to ha-rass the foe in the rear — Or to take a re-doubt, they would al-ways send out. For Ab-dal-lah Bul-bul A-meer —

Canto II
The Ruthless Russian

There are heroes in plenty and well known to fame
  In the army that's led by the Czar
But none were so brave as a man by the name
  Of Ivan Potschjinski Skidar.
He could imitate Toole, play the eucher and pool
  And perform on the Spanish guitar.
In fact quite the cream of the Muscovite team
  Was Ivan Potschjinski Skidar.

Canto III
The Encounter

One morning the Russian had shouldered his gun
  And assumed his most truculent sneer
And was walking down town when he happened to run
  Into Abdallah Bulbul Ameer.
'Young man,' says Bulbul, 'can your life be so dull
  That you're anxious to end your career?
For infidel know you have trod on the toe
  Of Abdallah Bulbul Ameer.'

50

Canto IV
The Challenge

'Take your ultimate look upon sunshine and brook
    Make your latest remarks on the war,
Which I mean to imply that you're going to die
    Mr Count Caskowhisky Cigar.'
Said the Russian, 'My friend your remarks in the end
    Would only be wasted I fear
For you'll never survive to repeat them alive
    Mr Abdallah Bulbul Ameer.'

Canto V
The Duel To The Death

Then the bold Mameluke drew his deadly chibouque
    And shouted 'Il Allah Ackbar'
And being intent upon slaughter he went
    For Ivan Potschjinski Skidar
But just as his knife had abstracted his life,
    In fact he was shouting 'Huzza',
When he found he was stuck by that subtle Calmuck,
    Young Ivan Potschjinski Skidar.

Canto VI
The Requiem

The consul drove up in a red crescent fly
    To give the survivor a cheer.
He arrived just in time to exchange a goodbye
    With Abdallah Bulbul Ameer.
And Skobeleff, Gourko, and Gortschakoff too
    Drove up on the Emperor's car
But all they could do was cry 'Och-whilliloo'
    For Ivan Potschjinski Skidar.

Canto VII
The Lonely Grave

There's a grave where the waves of the blue Danube roll
    And on it in characters clear
Is 'Stranger remember to pray for the soul
    Of Abdallah Bulbul Ameer.'
And a Muscovite maiden her vigil doth keep
    By the light of the true lover's star
And the name that she murmurs so oft in her sleep
    Is Ivan Potschjinski Skidar.

Abdul Abulbul Ameer
(Pirated version of original)

The sons of the Prophet are brave man and bold
And quite unaccustomed to fear
But the bravest by far in the ranks of the Shah
Was Abdul Abulbul Ameer.
Now the heroes were plenty and well-known to fame
In the troops that were led by the Czar
But the bravest of these was a man by the name
Of Ivan Skivinsky Skivar.

One day this bold Russian had shouldered his gun
And donned his most truculent sneer.
Down town he did go, where he trod on the toe
Of Abdul Abulbul Ameer.
'Young Man,' quote Abdul, 'Has life grown so dull
That you wish to end your career?
Vile infidel, know you have trod on the toe
Of Abdul Abulbul Ameer.'

Said Ivan, 'My friend, your remarks in the end
Will avail you but little, I fear,
For you ne'er will survive to repeat them alive,
Mr Abdul Abulbul Ameer.'
'So take your last look at sunshine and brook
And send your regrets to the Czar –
For by this, I imply, you are going to die,
Count Ivan Skivinsky Skivar.'

Now this bold Mameluke drew his trusty skibouk
With a cry of 'Allah Akbar'
And with murd'rous intent he ferociously went
For Ivan Skivinsky Skivar.

They fought all that night 'neath the pale yellow moon
The din it was heard from afar.
Huge multitudes came, so great was the fame
Of Abdul and Ivan Skivar.

As Abdul's long knife was extracting the life
(In fact he was shouting 'Huzza')
He felt himself struck by that wily calmuck,
Count Ivan Skivinsky Skivar.
The Sultan drove by in his red-breasted fly
Expecting the victor to cheer
But he only drew nigh to hear the last sigh
Of Abdul Abulbul Ameer.

Czar Petrovitch, too, in his spectacles blue
Drove up in his new-crested car
He arrived just in time to exchange a last line
With Ivan Skivinsky Skivar.
A Muscovite Maiden her lone vigil keeps
By the light of a pale polar star,
And the name that she murmurs so oft as she weeps
Is Ivan Skivinsky Skivar.

Now a tomb rises up where the Blue Danube flows
And engraved there in character clear
Is, 'Stranger, when passing, please pray for the soul
Of Abdul Abulbul Ameer.'

The Fortunes of Finnegan

Words by
PERCY FRENCH

Music by
HOUSTON COLLISSON

When Peter grew up big an' brown, a blacksmith he was made,
An' not a man in all the town could beat him at his trade,
One day to chase some corner boys he rushed out of his shed,
A motor-car was passin' an' it struck him on the head.

Chorus:

Says Branagan to Flanagan, an' Flanagan to Lanagan,
'I hear that Peter Finnegan has gone to glory clean.'
But brawny Peter Finnegan's a horrid man to rin agin –
They found that Peter Finnegan was mendin' the machine.

The boys in all the Barony were courtin' Mary Flynn,
An' no one but that Finnegan would have a chance to win.
All the others when they'd meet her 'bout the dowry would begin;
'But I'll take you, girl,' says Peter, 'In the clothes you're standin' in!'

(Music reproduced by permission of Dathi Music)

Chorus:

Says Branagan to Flanagan, an' Flanagan to Lanagan,
'It isn't Peter Finnegan she'll honour an' obey.'
But sorra a man but Finnegan will flirt wid Mary Flynn agin,
For bruisin' Peter Finnegan she married yesterday.

'Twas politics that Finnegan would study day an' night;
He'd argue right was mostly wrong an' black was really white.
And when the next election came the posters on the wall
Read, 'Vote for Peter Finnegan and the divil a tax at all!'

Chorus:

Says Branagan to Flanagan, an' Flanagan to Lanagan,
'The vote that Peter votes himself his only vote will be.'
But Finnegan can win again, no matter who he's in agin,
And bruisin' Peter Finnegan is Finnegan M.P.

Rowel Friers

55

Rafferty's Racin' Mare

Words by
PERCY FRENCH

Music by
HOUSTON COLLISSON

I was the jockey they chose to ride,
And often the owner he'd sware
That there wasn't a leap in the world too wide
To baffle the racin' mare.
Over hurdle and ditch, she went like a witch
Till she came where the water shone.
I gave her head, but she stopp'd at it dead
She stopped, and I went on.

56

Chorus:

Oh! Rafferty's racin' mare!
I whirtled through the air,
Like a beautiful bird
But nivver a word
From Rafferty's racin' mare.
Oh! Rafferty's racin' mare!
The bhoys cried out take care,
I took all I could
But it wasn't much good
To me nor the racin' mare.

'Get up, you lad,' says Ballinafad,
'You'll win the race for us yet.'
But I didn't care for the look of the mare,
Nor the way that her legs were set.
Says they, 'The horse'll stay the course,
She'll stay it ivry foot.'
'You're right, ' says I – 'I don't deny,
She'll stay just where she's put.'

Chorus:

Oh! Rafferty's racin' mare!
We danced around her there,
With stones and sticks, and bits o' bricks,
We hit her fair and square,
Oh! Rafferty's racin' mare!
The field they leap't it there,
And there on the brink, she'd stand and drink,
Would Rafferty's racin' mare.

But where was Rafferty all the time,
Oh! Rafferty! he's the lad,
There in the ring – he stood like a king,
Cheerin' the mare like mad.
His brother was there, disguised, of course,
As a Roosian millionaire,
Giving the odds against every horse,
And the longest against the mare.

Chorus:

Oh! Rafferty's racin' mare!
'Twas more than we could bear,
When a bookie revealed
He was backin' the field,
Instead of the racin' mare.
We've got the day to spare,
We've got the millionaire;
And we're havin' a race around the place,
And Rafferty – he's the hare.

57

The Darlin' Girl from Clare

Words and music by
PERCY FRENCH

Sez Fagin, ''Tis the father I'll be plazin'
I'll tell him of the land I've tilled,
I'll tell him of the cattle I have grazin'
And the house I mean to build;
And whin he sees the 'arable' and 'pasture'

And the fat stock feedin' there,
An' the hens an' the chickens,
Ye may go to the dickens
For the girl from the County Clare.'

Chorus:

So every man had got the finest plan
Ye ever see now – barrin' me now,
Ev'ry day there's one of them would say
That she'll agree now – you'll see now
Thinks I, 'Well now
Though I haven't ere a cow
Of brass I've got my share,
And so I know the way they ought to go
About the darlin' girl from Clare.'

Sez Sharkey, 'She'll be coming to the shop here
To buy some sort of thing,
I'll axe her if she has a mind to stop here,
And should I buy the ring:
An' whin she sees the curtains on the windas,
An' the old clock on the stair
Keepin' time to the minit,
No one else will be in it
With the darlin' girl from Clare!'

Chorus:

So every man had got the finest plan
Ye ever see now – barrin' me now,
Ev'ry day there's one of them would say,
That she'll agree now – you'll see now,
Thinks I, 'Ye may stop
All yer life in yer shop,
An' not a hair I'll care,
Wid all yer gold
Ye'll never hold a hold
Upon the darlin' girl from Clare.'

I never said a single word about her,
But I met the girl that day,
I told her I could never live widout her,
An' what had she to say?
She said that I might go and see her father:
I met him then and there,
An' in less than an hour
We were fightin' for the dower
Of the darlin' girl from Clare!

Chorus:

So every man had got the finest plan
Ye ever see now – barrin' me now,
Ev'ry day there's one of them would say
That she'll agree now – you'll see now;
But late last night
When the moon was bright
I axed her if she'd share
Me joy an' me sorra –
An' begorra! on tomorra
I'll be married to the girl from Clare!

Rowel Friers

60

The Darlin' Girl from Clare

(Ladies' Version)

I haven't any rights to be complaining
Wid three strings to my bow,
I declare to you it's lovers it is raining!
On every bush they grow;
I'm told they talk about me night and morning,
And every boy will swear,
'There's not a pearl in the wide, wide worl'
Like the girl from the County Clare!'

Chorus:

And ev'ry man has got the finest plan
Ye ever see now – 'bout me now,
Ev'ry day there's one of them would say
That she'll agree now – you will see now;
All night they'll fight
As to which has got the right
My property to share
But oh! boys oh!
That's not the way to go,
To win the darlin' girl from Clare.

Sez Phelim, ''Tis the father I'll be plazin'
I'll tell him of the land I've tilled,
I'll tell him of the cattle I have grazin'
And the house I mean to build;
And whin he sees the 'arable' and 'pasture'
And the fat stock feedin' there,
An' the hens an' the chickens,
Ye may go to the dickens
For the girl from the County Clare.'

Chorus:

So every man had got the finest plan
Ye ever see now – 'bout me now,
Ev'ry day there's one of them would say
That she'll agree now – you'll see now;
Thinks I, 'You're grand,
Wid your house and your land,'
But I'm not wanting there,
For oh! boys oh!
That's not the way to go
About the darlin' girl from Clare.

Sez Connor, 'She'll be coming to the shop here
To buy some sort of thing,
I'll axe her if she has a mind to stop here,
And should I buy the ring;
An' whin she sees the curtains on the windas,
An' the old clock on the stair
Keepin' time to the minit,
No one else will be in it
With the darlin' girl from Clare.'

Chorus:

So every man had got the finest plan
Ye ever see now — 'bout me now,
Ev'ry day there's one of them would say
That she'll agree now — you'll see now
Thinks I, 'Ye may stop
Till yer dead in yer shop
An' not a hair I'll care,
Wid all your gold
Ye'll never hold a hold
Upon the darlin' girl from Clare.'

But Seamus came and put his arms about me,
Oh! He's the right boy, too,
He told me he could never live without me,
And so what could I do!
I told him he must go and see me father,
He kissed me then and there,
And in less than an hour
He was fighting for the dower
Of the darlin' girl from Clare.

Chorus:

So ev'ry man had got the finest plan
Ye ever see now — 'bout me now,
Ev'ry day there's one of them would say
That she'll agree now — you'll see now;
But late last night
When the moon was bright
He axed me if I'd share
His joy an' his sorra —
An' begorra! on tomorra
He'll be married to the girl from Clare!

62

'Ach, I Dunno!'

Words by
PERCY FRENCH

Music by
MOLLY H. FRENCH

The convent is in a commotion
   To think of me taking a spouse,
And they wonder I hadn't the notion
   Of taking the vows.
'Tis a beautiful life and a quiet,
   And keeps ye from going below,
As a girl I thought I might try it,
   But, ach, I dunno!

I've none but meself to look after,
   An' marriage it fills me with fears,
I think I'd have less of the laughter
   And more of the tears.
I'll not be a slave like me mother,
   With six of us all in a row,
Even one little baby's a bother,
   But, ach, I dunno!

There's a lad that has taken me fancy,
   I know he's a bit of a limb,
And though marriage is terrible chancy,
   I'd – chance it with him.
He's coming to-night – oh – I tingle
   From the top of me head to me toe,
I'll tell him I'd rather live single,
   But, ach, I dunno!

*(Music reproduced by permission of
EMI Music Publishing Ltd.)*

The Oklahoma Rose

Words and music by
PERCY FRENCH

64

All through de day she keeps lookin' down demurely,
   'Much as to say, 'I can't be a woman surely!
I still can play with my doll securely,
   For dis ain't de time to spoon.'
But when de sun am sinkin' her eyes begin a winkin'
   An' I know she's thinkin' of dis yer coloured coon.
Oh! Ain't I glad I found her, in love chains I have bound her,
   Her face is rather rounder, it's rounder than de moon.

    Repeat Chorus

She hears me call an' she comes a-creepin', creepin',
   Over de wall she sees me leapin', leapin',
Big folks an' small quietly are sleepin',
   When I meet ma lily belle.
Up an' down de ladder I'm slippin' like a shadder,
   No one could be gladder dan me, I don't suppose.
Oh! Ain't I glad I found her, in true love I have bound her,
   Her face is rather rounder, it's rounder dan de moon.

    Repeat Chorus

Inishmeela

Words by
PERCY FRENCH

Music by
PHILIP GREEN

I can on-ly see the moonbeams that on In-ish-mee-la float, But if I slept in-side the fair-ies ring. I could see them sail-ing, sail-ing in their lit-tle sil-ver boat, And I'd hear the song the lit-tle peo-ple sing. For the fai-ry man has told me how he slumbered there one day, and a-woke to find them dancing on the shore, And still he hears them singing, though 'tis faint and far a-way, And he's wishing he was with them ev-er-more. I've seen the Queen of fai-ry land, I've heard her wond'rous song, With her the heights of hap-pi-ness I've flown, Now I know that days are wea-ry, now I know that nights are long, For the one I love has left me all a-lone. In-ish-mee-la, In-ish-mee-la, There's a sleep that knows no dream, And it's in that dreamless slumber I shall be, For I know that I shall wa-ken by some still ce-les-tial stream And through the gold-en light she'll come to me.

(Music reproduced by permission of
EMI Music Publishing Ltd.)

Cornelius Burke

Words and music by
PERCY FRENCH

Wait for a While Now, Mary

Words by
PERCY FRENCH

Music by
HOUSTON COLLISSON

Says I, 'Bye-the-bye,
Did you hear in Athy
What Hennessy got for his cow?'
Says she, 'Do you know
That you haven't let go
Of my hand since you took it just now?'
'Well I can't understand
What came over my hand
To be squeezing your fingers like that.'
Says she, 'I must go
It's not proper, you know!'
But I said as she straightened her hat,

(Music reproduced by permission of Dathi Music)

'Wait for a while now, Mary,
I've something more to say;
Wait for a while now, Mary,
You needn't run away.'
'Oh, it's all very fine,' says Mary,
'I'm wasting all my day.'
Says I, 'That's true –
I'll waste mine too.'
That's all I found to say.

Says I, 'There's a mare
In the meadow down there
Worth forty – I wouldn't take less.'
Says she, in some haste,
'Oh, your arm's round my waist
And it's spoiling the sit of my dress!'
'Now, how in the world
My arum got curled –
I'll try to explain to you Miss.'
Says she, 'Don't explain,
For it's perfectly plain
I'd better be home out of this!'

Chorus:
'Wait for a while now, Mary
I know what I've to say;
Wait for a while now, Mary
You've stole my heart away!'
'Did it not meet mine?' says Mary
'It passed yours on the way!'
'Oh tabhair 'm pog
Ma Colleen og!'
That's all I found to say.

Bad Ballads for Baddish Babes

I
The Absolutely Unanswerable

Words by
PERCY FRENCH

Music by
HOUSTON COLLISSON

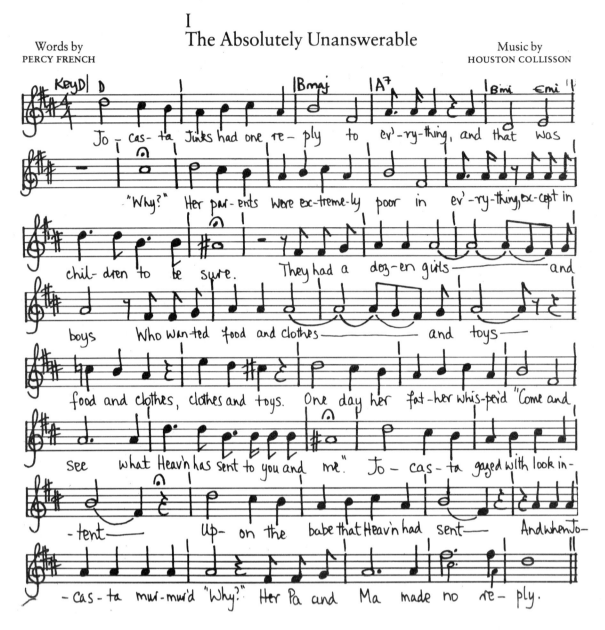

II
The Frankly Homicidal

The par-ents of the Tomp-kins kid were taught to do as they were bid. And as the kid was fond of strife They led a some-what harr-ass'd life. One day he or-der'd them to die, They did so al-most in-stant-ly. For in the ri-ver's gent-le breast They found a great-ly need-ed rest.

One (Spoken) found them — Mr. and Mrs Tompkins

morn-ing to the kid's de-spair, He "Wrong side up with care!"

71

III
The Infantile Tyrannical

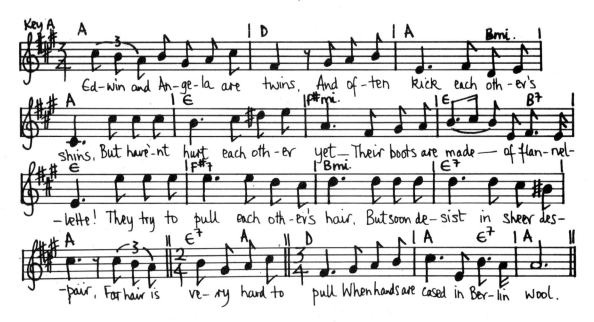

IV
The Tactfully Paternal

72

'The Hoodoo'

Words by
PERCY FRENCH

Music by
HOUSTON COLLISSON

Work at night for dose we luv –
Dat scares de Hoodoo!
Den him sings like a turtle dove, cooin' all night long,
Now dat we're one dat's what we do do,
Guess it's what I see ma Lindy Loo do
Wish for de little one dat we've got
Singin' de whole night thro'.

Chorus:

So I know,
When twilight shades are falling
Comes the foe de picaninnies dread,
Soft and slow I hear de Hoodoo calling:
'Are dere any little picaninnies who am not in bed?'

73

Flaherty's Drake

Words and music by
PERCY FRENCH

That night when in bed
In the loft overhead
The door of the shed
Gave a kind of a crake –
'Get up man!' says Biddy –
That's Flaherty's widdy –
'I think 'tis the voice of Ned Flaherty's drake.'
Now with that remark
I leapt up like a lark
And ran in the dark
To the shores of the lake;
And there 'twas I found it,
Its four wives around it;
Some blackguard had drownded
Ned Flaherty's drake.

74

Chorus:

Quack, quack, quack, went the ducks upon his track,
As they followed him down to the shore;
They may quack, quack, quack, but he's never comin' back
No, he's never comin' back no more.

I made such a din
That the neighbours came in:
Says Councillor Flynn,
'Deypositors I'll take.
Build up a large fire
And then we'll enquire
What caused the demayse of Ned Flaherty's drake.'
When the coroner sat
On the bird, says he, 'Pat,
'Tis tender and fat
What a meal it would make.'
And then, never mindin'
The tears my eyes blindin',
They roasted and dined on
Ned Flaherty's drake.

Repeat Chorus

Phil the Fluter's Ball

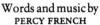

Words and music by
PERCY FRENCH

There was Misther Denis Dogherty, who kep' the runnin' dog;
There was little crooked Paddy, from the Tiraloughett bog;
There were boys from every Barony, and girls from ev'ry 'art'
And the beautiful Miss Bradys, in their private ass an' cart,
And along with them came bouncin' Mrs Cafferty,
Little Micky Mulligan was also to the fore,
Rose, Suzanne, and Margaret O'Rafferty,
The flower of Ardragullion, and the pride of Petravore.

Repeat Chorus

First, little Micky Mulligan got up to show them how,
And then the Widda' Cafferty steps out and makes her bow,
'I could dance you off your feet,' sez she, 'as sure as you are born,
If ye'll only make the piper play "The hare was in the corn".'
So Phil plays up to the best of his ability,
The lady and the gentleman begin to do their share;
'Faith then Mick it's you that has agility!'
'Arrah! Begorra Mrs Cafferty, yer leppin' like a hare!'

Repeat Chorus

Then Phil the Fluther tipped a wink to little Crooked Pat,
'I think it's nearly time,' sez he, 'for passin' round the hat.'
So Paddy pass'd the caubeen round, and looking mighty cute
Sez, 'Ye've got to pay the piper when he toothers on the flute.'
Then all joined in wid the greatest joviality,
Coverin' the buckle, and the shuffle, and the cut;
Jigs were danced of the very finest quality,
But the Widda' bate the company at 'handling the fut'.

Repeat Chorus

Rowel Friers

77

Andy McElroe

Words by
PERCY FRENCH

Music by
JOHN ROSS

1. My bro-ther An-dy said that for a sol-dier he would go, So great ex-cite-ment came up-on the house of Mc-El- roe. My fa-ther sold a bog-hole to e- quip him for the war, And my mo-ther sold the cush-ions of her Sun-day jaunt-ing car. And when brave An-dy reach'd the front, 'Twas fur-ious work he made They ap--point-ed him a pri-vate in the Croc-o-dile Bri- gade. The sound of An-dy's bat-tle cry struck ter-ror thro' the foe, His foot was on the des-ert and his name was Mc-El- roe. At least that's what the let-ters said that came a-cross the foam, To An-dy's an-xious re-la-tives a- wait-ing him at home. The pa-pers say he ran a-way be--fore he saw the foe, But that was quite un-like the style of An-dy Mc-El- roe.

78

One morning brave Lord Wolseley for a battle felt inclined;
But all could see the General had something on his mind;
Sez he, 'My staff, 'twere dangerous to face yon deadly foe,
Unless we're sure that quite prepared is Andy McElroe.'
Then Andy cried, 'I'm here, my Lord, and ready for the fray.'
'Advance then,' cried Lord Wolseley, 'and let every trumpet bray.'
Then England, Ireland, Scotland, rolled together on the foe,
But far ahead of everyone rushed Andy McElroe.

Chorus:

At least, that's what the letter said that came across the foam
To Andy's anxious relatives, awaiting him at home.
The Government despatches had another tale – but no!
We won't believe a word against brave Andy McElroe.

The Mahdi had gone up a tree, a spyglass in his eye,
To see his Paynim chivalry the Northern Prowess try:
But soon he saw a form of dread, and cried in tones of woe,
'Be jabbers let me out of this – there's Andy McElroe!'
Then down he hurried from his tree, and straight away he ran,
To keep appointments, so he said, in distant Kordofan,
And fled those Arab soldiery like sand siroccos blow,
Pursued (with much profanity) by Andy McElroe.

Chorus:

At least, that's what he told us when returning o'er the foam
To greet his anxious relatives, awaiting him at home.
So sing the song of triumph, and let all your bumpers flow,
In honour of our countryman, brave Andrew McElroe.

Rowel Friers

79

Maguire's Motor Bike
(A Tragedy in Four Acts)

Words by
PERCY FRENCH

Music by
HOUSTON COLLISSON

1. It was Mick Maguire— made it All a- lone and all un-aid-ed, For I tell you that a brain-y boy was Mick. And for div-il-mint and mur- ther, Faith you need'-n't go no fur-ther Than the bi-cy-cle he call'd "The Kill me quick!" Oh, the gear-case was a ket-tle Made of good Brit-an-nia met-al, As good as you would buy in an-y shop, And when once you set it go-in' Faith there nev-er was no know-in Where Ma-guire's— mot-or bi-cy-cle would stop. But the bike's all right Not a bit it mat-ter'd For the bike's all right And none the worse for wear. Oh, the bike's all-right The rid-er might be shat-ter'd But the bike's all-right So Ma-guire doesn't care.

'Twould come whizzin' round a corner,
  And before you'd time to warn her
'Twould be through some poor old woman like a knife;
  And Flynn, the undertaker,
  Said to Mick (that was the maker),
That he never was so busy in his life.
  He'd lend it to relations
  From whom he'd expectations,
And to folks for whom he didn't care;
  Then Mick would say with sorrow,
  'There'll be funerals tomorrow,'
And it somehow always happened that there were.

  Chorus:

  But the bike's all right,
  His uncle tried to cycle,
  Oh! the bike's all right,
  And none the worse for wear.
  The bike's all right,
  The money went to Michael,
  Oh! the bike's all right,
  So Maguire doesn't care.

They tried him for manslaughter,
  But the case would not hold water,
For Maguire proved an alibi each time;
  And not a one could shake him,
  And divil a one could make him
In any ways accessory to crime.
  They were gettin' quite alarmed,
  And so a plot was formed,
A conspiracy they thought would never fail;
  So they sought the level crossin'
  When the 'nine o'clock' was passin',
And they laid it gintly down upon the rail.

  Chorus:

  Oh! the bike's all right,
  Not a bit it mattered,
  Oh! the bike's all right,
  And none the worse for wear.
  The bike's all right,
  The 'nine o'clock' was scattered,
  But the bike's all right,
  So Maguire doesn't care.

Oh! the town was in a fury,
    For at the next grand jury
They were fined for an attempt to wreck the train,
    And out of the entire lot
    'Twas only Mick Maguire got
Away from out the court without a stain.
    So they held a monster meetin'
    For the purpose of debatin'
A way to put the cycle on the shelf;
    So at last it was decided,
    And assinted, and provided,
That Maguire takes a ride on it himself.

    Chorus:

    Oh! the bike's all right,
    Maguire tried to ride it.
    Oh! the bike's all right,
    Just as it was before.
    The bike's all right,
    They buried it beside him,
    The bike's all right,
    But Maguire he's no more.

Little Bridget Flynn

Words by
PERCY FRENCH

Music by
MOLLY H. FRENCH

Now, me father often tells me I should go and have a try
To get a girl that owns a bit of land;
I know the way he says it that there's someone in his eye,
And me mother has the whole thing planned.
Maybe so, I dunno,
And 'twould melify them greatly to agree,
But there's little Brigid Flynn,
Sure it's her I want to win,
Though she never throws an eye at me.

Now there's a little girl who is worth her weight in gold,
An' that's a dacent dowry don't you see;
So I think I'll go and ask her just as soon as I get bold,
If she'll come and have an eye to me.
Will she go – I dunno,
But I'd love to have her sittin' on me knee,
And I'd sing like a thrush
On a hawthorn bush,
If she'd come and have an eye to me.

Eileen Oge

Words by
PERCY FRENCH

Music by
HOUSTON COLLISSON

Friday at the Fair of Ballintubber,
Eileen met McGrath, the cattle-jobber,
I'd like to lave me mark upon the robber
For he stole away the Pride of Petravore.
He never seem'd to see the girl at all,
Even when she ogled him from underneath her shawl,
Lookin' big and masterful, while she was looking small,
Most provokin' for the Pride of Petravore.

84

Eileen Oge, me heart is growin' grey
Ever since the day you wander'd far away.
Eileen Oge, there's good fish in the say,
But there's no one like the Pride of Petravore.

So it went as it was in the beginning,
Eileen Oge was bent upon the winning.
Big McGrath contentedly was grinning,
Being courted by the Pride of Petravore.
Sez he, 'I know a girl that could knock you into fits.'
At that Eileen nearly lost her wits.
The upshot of the ruction was that now the robber sits,
With his arm around the Pride of Petravore.

Repeat Chorus

Boys oh boys! with fate 'tis hard to grapple,
Of my eye 'tis Eileen was the apple.
And now to see her walkin' to the chapel
Wid the hardest featured man in Petravore.
And, now, me boys, this is all I have to say,
When you do your courtin' make no display,
If you want them to run after you just walk the other way,
For they're mostly like the Pride of Petravore.

Repeat Chorus

Kitty Gallagher

Words and music by
PERCY FRENCH

Key Cmi—E♭maj.

1. Oh I've court-ed many a one, And me heart has been un-done, So of - ten that ye'd think that it was gone o' me — But faith I know 'tis there Since I first was made a-ware of beau-ti-ful Miss Kit-ty's phy-si-on-o-my. Talk of Ve-nus! she was no way her su-per-i-or Talk of Li-ly Lang-try! she would sing un-com-mon small! Ma-ry Ann McGill-i-gan was ev-'ry way in-fer-i-or Pret-ty Kit-ty Gal-lagh-er's the dar-lin' of them all. Pret-ty Kit-ty Gal-lagh-er sure and I could swal-low her, She'd be cream and su-gar in me tay. Oh! Pret-ty Kit-ty Gal-lagh-er, faith, and I could fol-low her, Ov-er all the world and a-way.

I fought the whole townland,
And the Finn McCool brass band,
Who thought they had a sort of prior claim to her;
But with me keppeen in me hand,
Faith I made them understand
That Brady was the man to give a name to her.
Mick McCoogan would persuade me to surrender her,
Now he finds it difficult to use a brush and comb,
I dunno if his head or if his heart is now the tenderer:
We fought for pretty Kitty till the cows were coming home.

    Chorus:

    Pretty Kitty Gallagher, sure and I could swallow her,
    She'd be cream and sugar in me tay:
    Oh! Pretty Kitty Gallagher, faith, and I could follow her,
    Over all the world and away.

Of no man was I afraid;
But they made an ambuscade;
A course that would have paralysed Napoleon;
But before they laid me out
Faith I caught them many a clout,
You wouldn't find a head but was a holey 'un!
When Miss Kitty seen the broken-headed regiment,
Paradin' out in front of her and askin' her to wife,
Kneelin' down beside me corp the duck of diamonds said she meant
To take the man they murdered and that brought me back to life!

    Repeat Chorus

Mulligan's Masquerade

Words and music by
PERCY FRENCH

Bedalia Crow was 'Beautiful Snow'
And it made a curious blend;
O'Hollighan wasn't invited, so
He came as an 'Absent Friend';
That boy of Magee's was 'Mefishtofeles',
But we called a spade a spade,
And not bein' civil, we called him 'The Divil'
At Mulligan's Masquerade.

And Hennissy came as a 'Highwayman'
In the hat that his father wore,
They say that's the way that the father begun
Amassin' his little store;
Miss Fay was seen as a 'Fairy Queen',
In a gauzy skirt arrayed;
We had to keep her behind the screen
At Mulligan's Masquerade.

Miss Foxey Farrell was the 'Queen of France'
And the sight I never shall forget,
When Hogan, as 'Hamlet', begged a dance,
From 'Maeryanne Toinette';
Mrs Regan came as a 'Woodland Elf',
I don't know what she weighed,
But her very first prance broke all the delft,
At Mulligan's Masquerade.

Chorus:

Miss Casey, as 'Cycling' took the floor
In a corderoys and a kilt;
Her father patched up the old cuttamore
And came as a 'Crazy Quilt';
Miss Mullaby as 'Joan of Cork'
Her beautiful shape displayed;
Faith! many a scarecrow you'd remark
At Mulligan's Masquerade.

Jim Wheelahan's Automobeel

Words by
PERCY FRENCH

Music by
HOUSTON COLLISSON

1. When Jim Wheel-a-han made all his mon-ey in trade, He said he'd as-ton-ish the town — And he stuck to his word, as you'll say when you've heard Of the won-der-ful yoke he brought down — 'Twas the lat-est de-sign in the mot-or-car line, Pa-ris-ian and ve-ry gen-teel — A mot-or might do for me or for you, But this was an Au-to-mo-beel! — Jim Wheel-a-han's Au-to-mo-beel! — Oh, that was the Tath-e-rin wheel — He tel-e-graph'd down he would ride thro' the town Next day in his Au-to-mo-beel! —

A Sailor Courted
(Come-All-Ye)

Words by
PERCY FRENCH

Music by
BRENDAN O'DOWDA

But the farmer's daughter had great possessions,
A silver teapot and two pounds in gold;
And says she, 'Would ye marry me, me bould salt water sea-sailor,
If I threw them into the ocean cold?'

'Oh,' says he, 'I'd marry you, me heart's enchantment,
If you had nothing but your father's curse!'
So she made up a bundle of all her grand possessions,
and threw them into the water. . . that ends that verse.

But the sailor he could swim like a duckling,
So into the water he dived down deep below,
Got hold of the bundle and swam away chuckling,
To think of the times he'd be having when he landed down in Ballinasloe.

But the farmer's daughter was kilt with the laughing,
To think of the bundle she'd made up out of a stone. . .
Oh! a sailor courted a farmer's daughter,
But now he's wishing that he'd left the girl alone.

(Music reproduced by permission of Dathi Music)

91

Come Back, Paddy Reilly

Words and music by
PERCY FRENCH

1. The gar-den of Ed-en is van-ish'd they say, But I know the lie of it still —— Just turn to the left at the bridge of Fin-ea And stop when half-way to Coote-hill —— 'Tis there I will find it, I know sure e-nough, When for-tune has come to my call —— Oh the grass it is green a-round Bal-ly-james-duff, And the blue sky is ov-er it all —— And tones that are ten-der, and tones that are gruff, Are whis-per-ing ov-er the sea —— "Come back Pad-dy Reil-ly to Bal-ly-james-duff, Come home Pad-dy Reil-ly to me—"

My mother once told me that when I was born,
The day that I first saw the light,
I looked down the street on that very first morn,
and gave a great crow of delight.
Now most new born babies appear in a huff
And start with a sorrowful squall,
But I knew I was born in Ballyjamesduff,
And that's why I smiled on them all.
The baby's a man now, he's toil-worn and tough,
Still, whispers come over the sea,
'Come back, Paddy Reilly, to Ballyjamesduff,
Come home, Paddy Reilly, to me.'

The night that we danced by the light of the moon,
Wid Phil to the fore with his flute.
When Phil threw his lip over 'Come again soon'
He'd dance the foot out o' yer boot!
The day that I took long Magee by the scruff,
For slanderin' Rosie Kilrain,
Then marchin' him straight out of Ballyjamesduff
Assisted him into a drain.
Oh, sweet are me dreams, as the dudeen I puff,
Of whisperings over the sea,
'Come back, Paddy Reilly, to Ballyjamesduff,
Come home, Paddy Reilly, to me.'

I've loved the young women of every land –
That always came easy to me,
Just barrin' the belles of the Black-a-moor brand
And the chocolate shapes of Feegee.
But that sort of love is a moonshiny stuff
And never will addle me brain,
For the bells will be ringin' in Ballyjamesduff,
For me and me Rosie Kilrain!
And all through their glamour, their gas, and their guff,
A whisper comes over the sea,
'Come back, Paddy Reilly, to Ballyjamesduff,
Come home, Paddy Reilly, to me.'

Gortnamona

Words by
PERCY FRENCH

Music by
PHILIP GREEN

Long, long ago, in the woods of Gortnamona,
   I thought the wind was sighing round the blackthorn tree;
But oh! it was the banshee that was crying, crying, crying,
   And I knew my love was dying far across the sea.

Now if you go through the woods of Gortnamona,
   You'll hear the raindrops creeping through the blackthorn tree.
But oh! it is the tears I am weeping, weeping, weeping,
   For the loved one that is sleeping far away from me.

*(Music reproduced by permission of
EMI MusicPublishing Ltd.)*

94

Sweet Marie

Words by
PERCY FRENCH

Music by
BRENDAN O'DOWDA

Key F

1. There's a little racin' mare called Sweet Marie, And the temper of a bear has sweet marie, But I've backed the mare to win, And on her I've all me tin, So we'll take a trial spin Sweet marie. Hould yer holt, sweet marie, if ye bolt, sweet marie, Sure you'll never win the farmer's cup for me, And if you don't pull it thro', faith I'm done and so are you, For I'll trade you off for glue, Sweet Marie.

Now, the colours that I chose for Sweet Marie
Were lavender and rose for Sweet Marie,
Och, but now, no thanks to you, sure I'm quite another hue,
For I'm only black and blue, Sweet Marie.
    Hould your hoult, Sweet Marie,
    If you bolt, Sweet Marie,
    Sure, you'll never win the Farmers' Cup for me.
    Every daisy in the dell ought to know me mighty well,
    For on every one I fell, Sweet Marie.

Now we're started for the Cup, my Sweet Marie,
Weight for age and owners up, my Sweet Marie,
Owners up just now I own, but the way you're waltzing roun'
Sure, 'twill soon be owners down, Sweet Marie.
    Hould your hoult, Sweet Marie,
    Pass the colt, Sweet Marie.
    Och, you've gone and lost the Farmers' Cup for me,
    You're a stayer too, I find: but you're not the proper kind
    For you stay too far behind, Sweet Marie.

(Music reproduced by permission of Dathi Music)

McBreen's Heifer

Words and music by
PERCY FRENCH

Entirely bothered was Jamesy O'Byrne,
He thought that he'd give the school-master a turn;
Sez he, 'To wed Kitty is very good fun,
But a heifer's a heifer when all's said an' done.
A girl she might lose her good looks any how —
And a heifer might grow to an elegant cow;
But still there's no price for the stock, d'ye mind.
And Jane has a face that the Divil designed.'

Repeat First Chorus

Now the school-master said, with a great deal of sense,
'We'll reduce the two girls to shillin's an' pence,
Add the price of the heifer then Jane I'll be bound
Will come out the top by a couple o' pound;
But still I'm forgettin' that down in Glengall
The stock is just goin' for nothin' at all.'
So Jim thought he'd wait till the end of the year,
Till girls might be cheaper or stock might be dear.

Chorus:

But when he came for Kitty, she was married to McVittie,
And McGee had appropriated Jane,
So whether there's the differ of the price of a heifer,
Is a thing that he never would explain.

'Are Ye Right There, Michael?'

A lay of the Wild West Clare

Words and music by
PERCY FRENCH

They find out where the engine's been hiding,
   And it drags you to sweet Corofin;
Says the guard, 'Back her down on the siding,
   There's the goods from Kilrush comin' in.'
Perhaps it comes in in two hours,
   Perhaps it breaks down on the way;
'If it does,' says the guard, 'be the powers,
   We're here for the rest of the day!'

   And while you sit and curse your luck,
   The train backs down into a truck!

'Are ye right there, Michael, are ye right?
Have ye got the parcel there for Mrs White?
   Ye haven't! Oh, begorra!
   Say it's comin' down tomorra –
And it might now, Michael, so it might!'

At Lahinch the sea shines like a jewel,
   With joy you are ready to shout,
When the stoker cries out, 'There's no fuel,
   And the fire's taytotally out.
But hand up that bit of a log there –
   I'll soon have ye out of the fix;
There's a fine clamp of turf in the bog there,
   And the rest go a-gatherin' sticks.'

   And while you're breakin' bits of trees,
   You hear some wise remarks like these:

'Are ye right there, Michael, are ye right?
Do ye think that ye can get the fire to light?'
   'Oh, an hour you'll require,
   For the turf it might be drier –'
'Well, it might now, Michael, so it might!'

Kilkee! Oh, you never get near it!
   You're in luck if the train brings you back,
For the permanent way is so queer, it
   Spends most of its time off the track.
Uphill the ould engine is climbin',
   While the passengers push with a will;
You're in luck when you reach Ennistymon,
   For all the way home is downhill.

   And as you're wobbling through the dark,
   You hear the guard make this remark:

'Are ye right there, Michael are ye right?
Do you think that ye'll be home before it's light?'
   ''Tis all dependin' whether
   The ould engine howlds together –'
'And it might now, Michael, so it might!'

That's Why We're Burying Him

Words by
PERCY FRENCH

Music by
ETTIE FRENCH

Mick Maguire join'd a choir
But the height of his desire
Was to sing the tenor solo in a concert hall.
He practised *Pagliacci*,
As he heard the airs were catchy,
The piano played a prelude, and he gave one bawl!

Chorus:

That's why we're burying him;
That's why the poor man's dead.
That's why we're hurrying him
Off to his last long bed.
One yelp! then cries for help,
As the eggs flew round his head;
That's why the poor man's dead.

Frisco Foss he stole a 'hoss'
And ere they strung him up, the boss
Said, 'If any girl will marry him, the man goes free,'
Then up came widow Twankey,
She was lean and she was lanky,
And says she, 'Kind sir, I'll thanky, hand him down to me.'

Chorus:

That's why we're burying him;
That's why the poor man's dead.
That's why we're hurrying him
Off to his last long bed.
One glance at his only chance,
Then, 'String me up!' he said;
That's why the poor man's dead.

Larry Mick McGarry

Words and music by
PERCY FRENCH

1. Oh! Lar-ry Mick Mc- Gar-ry was the tor- ment of the town. A
lad a wo-man's glad o' But a man would like to drown— With a
smile he would be-guile a-way a girl— from her boy— An be-
-fore he got a mile a-way he tired— of his toy.
Tith-er-y-ah the doo-dle ah As far as I can see—
Tith-er-y-ah the doo-dle ah No mar-ty-in' for me! —
Bright by the can-dle light an' pour-in' out the tea. But yer
glad ye did-nt ax her in the mom— ing ——.

Oh, Larry played old Harry
With the girls about the place,
At the dancin' they'd be glancin'
At the features of his face,
But he never would endeavour
To be lover-like until
Mary Carey, she's a fairy,
Had him goin' like a mill.

102

Titheryah the doodle ah
He met her in the street,
Titheryah the doodle ah
Sez he, 'Yer lookin' sweet.
A walk an' a talk wid you
I think would be a treat,'
But all he got from Mary was,
'Good morning!'

The dancin' down at Clancy's
Brought in all the neighbourhood,
Though the roof wasn't waterproof,
The floor was fairly good;
An' Larry Mick McGarry
He could handle well the leg,
But Mary, light an' airy,
Oh, she took him down a peg.

Chorus:

Titheryah the doodle ah
She footed it wid Flynn
Titheryah the doodle ah
An' all the other min.
But Larry Mick McGarry
Oh! he hadn't a look in,
Faith he had to go and find her
In the morning.

Oh, she taught him till she brought him
Up to where she had designed.
Sez Larry, 'Will ye marry me?'
Sez she, 'I wouldn't mind.'
He kissed her an' carrissed her,
Which is quite the proper thing,
Then together, hell for leather,
They were off to buy a ring.

Chorus:

Titheryah the doodle ah
'No marryin',' sez you,
Titheryah the doodle ah
Ye may escape the 'flu:
Wait till you meet yer mate
An' all there is to do
Is to go an' buy the licence
In the morning.

An Irish Mother

Words by
PERCY FRENCH

Music by
BRENDAN O'DOWDA

1. A — wee slip draw-in' wa-ter, Me oald man at the plough. No
grown up son nor daugh-ter, That's the way we've farm-in' now, "No —
work and lit-tle pleas-ure" Was the cry be-fore they wint Now they're
get-tin' both full meas-ure, So I ought to be con-tint.
Great wa-ges men is giv-in' In that land be-yant the say, But 'tis
lone-ly, lone-ly liv-in' Whin the child-her is a-way.

Och, the baby in the cradle,
    Blue eyes and curlin' hair,
God knows I'd give a gra'dle
    To have little Pether there;
No doubt he'd find it funny
    Lyin' here upon me arm,
Him – that's earnin' the good money,
    On a Californy farm.

Six pounds it was or sivin
    He sint last quarter day,
But 'tis lonely-lonely livin'
    Whin the childher is away.

*(Music reproduced by permission of
EMI Music Publishing Ltd.)*

God is good – no better,
  And the Divil might be worse,
Each month there comes a letther
  Bringing somethin' for the purse.
And me ould man's heart rejoices
  Whin he reads they're doin' fine,
But it's oh! to hear their voices,
  And to feel their hands in mine.

To see the cattle drivin'
  And the young ones makin' hay,
'Tis a lonely land to live in
  Whin the childher is away.

Whin the shadows do be fallin'
  On the ould man there an' me,
'Tis hard to keep from callin'
  'Come in, childher, to yer tea!'
I can almost hear them comin'
  Mary Kate and little Con –
Och! but I'm the foolish woman,
  Sure they're all grown up an' gone.

That their sins may be forgiven,
  And not wan go astray,
I doubt I'd stay in Heaven
  If them childher was away.

Ballymilligan
(The Old Woman Speaks)
A sequel to 'The Irish Mother'

Words by
PERCY FRENCH

Music by
MOLLY H. FRENCH

1. Back to Bal-ly-mil-li-gan, it's there that I would be Back to Bal-ly-mil-li-gan be-side the sil-ver sea. The wee white hou-ses peep-ing out to greet the dawn o' day, The lit-tle traw-lers creep-ing out to fish be-low the bay. Oh! If I had me will a-gain it's there that I would be, Far a-way in Bal-ly-mil-li-gan, be-side the sil-ver sea.

They've paid me passage over – I've a gran'child on me knee –
An' I'm living here in clover in the home they've made for me.
    But it hasn't got the charm an' it hasn't got the view
    Of the little hillside farm that my Danny brought me to.
Oh! to feel the thrill again when he was courting me
Back in Ballymilligan beside the silver sea.

I've been in Wanamakers, and in all the mighty stores,
That cover many acres and have forty diff'rent floors,
    But it's down to Katy Ryan I'd be trav'lin' in me shoes,
    To do me bit o' buyin' and to hear the neighbours' news.
To pay the weeshy bill again, for sugar and for tea –
Back in Ballymilligan beside the silver sea.

(Music reproduced by permission of
EMI Music Publishing Ltd.)

106

No doubt I'd find a change in it, for time goes rollin' on,
I fancy I'd feel strange in it, the old companions gone,
    But there is one that's sleeping there – the one that I love best,
    Some day I may be creeping there to lay me down to rest.
An' then the old grey hill again will shelter him and me –
Back in Ballymilligan beside the silver sea.

Father O'Callaghan

Words by
PERCY FRENCH

Music by
HOUSTON COLLISSON

Rosie Mulvany was bright as a bird,
I lov'd her, she didn't object,
But somehow I never could bring out the word,
That Rose had a right to expect.
I'd dream of her nightly, I'd dream she said 'Yes,'
Be daylight my courage was gone,
I wore to a shadow, so in my distress,
I went and I saw Father Con.

108

O Father O'Callaghan,
   Will the dream come true?
O Father O'Callaghan,
   What is a boy to do?
And Father O'Callaghan said, 'See here,
   You must call dressed in Sunday clothes.
Say to her this, "Will you marry me dear?"
   You can leave the rest to Rose.'

We talk'd one night of the glorious days,
   When Ireland led the van,
With scholars as thick as the stars in the sky
   And work for every man.
''Twill come again,' said Father Con,
   And his fertile fancy paints
The glorious day when the sun shines on
   A new Isle of the Saints.

O Father O'Callaghan,
   When will the dream come true?
O Father O'Callaghan,
   If anyone knows, 'tis you.
And Father O'Callaghan raised his head,
   And smil'd his humorsome smile,
'When ev'ry man learns to rule himself
   'Twill then be a saintly isle.'

Father O'Callaghan's dead and gone,
   This many and many a day –
But we haven't forgot you Father Con,
   And it keeps us from goin' astray.
And so at the last great earthquake shock,
   When the trumpet's soundin' clear,
He'll guide to their God the faithful flock,
   Who knew him and lov'd him dear.

O Father O'Callaghan,
   When will the dream come true?
O Father O'Callaghan,
   If anyone knows 'tis you!
And Father O'Callaghan says no word,
   For he's sleepin' softly yet,
And when the Archangel's voice is heard,
   We know that he won't forget.

Tullinahaw

Words by
PERCY FRENCH

Music by
HOUSTON COLLISSON

Oh they lay by the wall an' they kep' wide awake
    Till they saw a man haulin' a cow to the lake.
'Honest man, tell me now is that cow all your own?'
    'Is it me own a cow that's all skin and bone?
Sure she belongs to Widda Geraghty;
    Home I was drivin' her from charity.'
'Tell me,' says Flynn – with some hilarity,
    'Why are you comin' from Tullinahaw?'
An' Sergeant Kilray was heard for to say,
    'The case is suspeecious in ev-er-y way,'
And Flynn said he saw a breach of the law
    In drivin' a cow from Tullinahaw.

110

Oh the trial came on an' the prisoner swore
   He was doin' a neighbourly act an' no more,
For the cow was no use and Widda that day
   Had give him a bob to take it away.
'Stop!' said the Judge, 'You've made no case of it,
   That is a lie, sir, on the face of it,
Perjury too there's ev'ry trace of it,
   Years they'll miss you in Tullinahaw.'
And Sergeant Kilray and Constable Flynn,
   They made no delay in runnin' him in.
An' there for a year he sits in the straw
   Lamentin' the grandeurs of Tullinahaw.

When they brought back the cow, says the Widda 'Ochone!
   How I wish them police would leave people alone,
For if I could have proved the ould reptile was drown'd
   I'd ha' got compinsation – aye – nine or ten pound.
Instid of the money to help further me,
   Here the ould baste is back to bother me.
Whin John comes out I know he'll murder me,
   Gettin' him took in Tullinahaw.'
An' Sergeant Kilray and Constable Flynn,
   The both of them grey and elderly min,
Still tell how they brought back ordher an' law –
   'Tis a different story in Tullinahaw!

Rowel Friers

111

Phistlin' Phil McHugh

Words and music by
PERCY FRENCH

There's Thady of the Cows —
Sure you know 'Ten-acre Thady',
With his fine new slated house,
He'd make her quite the lady.
But Thady needn't stay,
And there's no use his intragin'
For her heart is far away —
'Tis wid Phil McHugh stravagin'.

Repeat First Chorus

112

There's Danny Michael Dan,
Who is six fut in his stockin's,
A very proper man,
But she never heeds his knockin's,
She'd keep him standin' there
For three-quarters of a minit,
But she's racin' like a hare
When she thinks that Phil is in it.

Repeat First Chorus

'Tis wisdom's golden rule
I do teach her till I tire,
That every girl's a fool,
Ay, and every man's a liar.
What's that, you say, you hear,
That's set you all a thrimbly?
'Tis but the wind I fear
That is phistlin' down the chimbly.

Chorus:

Oh, Mary, you're contrary –
Come in and bar the door;
What's that scufflin'? Phil, you ruffian;
Sure I knew he'd come, asthore.
She's been settin' there and frettin',
But now her grievin's o'er
And the singin' will be ringing'
In her heart once more.

Mrs Brady

Words by
PERCY FRENCH

Music by
HOUSTON COLLISSON

1. Ould Brad-y's gone to glo-ry and the wid-da has the land, And as she's good to look at, you can ea-sy un-der-stand, That el-i-gi-ble suit-ors from the town of Ath-en-ry, Put on their best em-bell-ish-ments and thought they'd have a try. Jim Flynn the stat-ion mas-ter's son, Tho' not in Bra-dy's set, Was kind e-nough to say to her one eve-ning when they met: "Miss-us Bra-dy! Just a whis-per! To your mourn-ing bid a-dieu! I know a fine young gen-tle-man who'd not ob-ject to you, My fa-mi-ly may cut me, But you're brass e-nough for two" "I—— know who has the brass" says Mis-sus Bra-dy "you've brass e-nough for three", says Mis-sus Bra-dy.

114

Pat Dempsey heard that Jimmy had been sent against the wall;
Says Pat, 'It's not gentility the widda wants at all.
But "pity is akin to love", as everybody knows.
I'll tell her how I've got no girl to wash or mend my clothes.'
He dressed up like a scarecrow that across a field was hung,
And this was the come-hither that came slipping off his tongue:

>   *Chorus*:
>
>   'Mrs Brady, just a whisper!
>   I'd be glad to marry you
>   For indeed I've none to help me
>   With the work I have to do;
>   And the victuals that they cook me
>   I can neither chop nor chew.'
>   'I would not suit the place,' says Mrs Brady.
>   'I'd never do the work,' says Mrs Brady.

Then little Francis Fogarty said, 'Women, old and young,
Have always been deluthered by the civil-spoken tongue;
I'll tell her that her cheeks are like the summer rose in bloom,
Her eyes are like two diamonds, and her breath is sweet perfume,'
So off he goes to call on her, all flattery and lies,
And this was how he started in to carry off his prize:

>   *Chorus*:
>
>   'Mrs Brady, just a whisper!
>   There is none as fair as you,
>   Your eyes are like two diamonds
>   Your lips are honey dew;
>   I'm certain you're an angel,
>   And it is from heaven you flew.'
>   'I believe you're off your head,' says Mrs Brady,
>   'You ought to see the vet,' says Mrs Brady.

When Flynn, who keeps the grocer's shop, and owns a bit o' land,
Came home and heard how Pat had got the back of Mary's hand,
Says he, 'Myself and Mary has been friends through thick and thin.'
So he put on all his Sunday clothes, and barbarised his chin;
He called on her that morning, she was very sweet and kind.
And this was how he hinted at the thoughts were in his mind:

>   *Chorus*:
>
>   'Mrs Brady, just a whisper!
>   Sure I don't know how to woo;
>   But I've got a growin' business,
>   And I've love enough for two;
>   So name the happy day,
>   And would tomorrow mornin' do?'
>   'Ah! Why not this afternoon?' says Mrs Brady.
>   'Sure, there's danger in delay!' says Mrs Brady.

Mat Hannigan's Aunt

Words and music by
PERCY FRENCH

Oh, she never could raise her voice,
She never was known to scold,
But when Hannigan's aunt sed, 'No, you can't,'
You did what you were told;
And if anyone answered back,
Oh, then his hair she'd domb,
'For all I want,' sez Hannigan's Aunt,
'Is peace in our happy home.'

Repeat Chorus

116

Oh, when she went to Court,
The A-de-congs in vain
Would fume and rant, for Hannigan's Aunt
Said, 'Boy let go me thrain!'
And when the Lard Leftinant
A kiss on her brow would imprint
'Oh no, you can't,' said Hannigan's Aunt
'Widout me pa's consint.'

Repeat Chorus

Oh, 'tis often we'd praise her up,
We'd laud her to the sky,
We'd all descant on Hannigan's Aunt,
And hope she never would die.
But still I'd like to add –
If Hannigan isn't about –
That whin we plant Mat Hannigan's Aunt,
We won't be too put out.

Repeat Chorus

The Mountains of Mourne

Words and music by
PERCY FRENCH

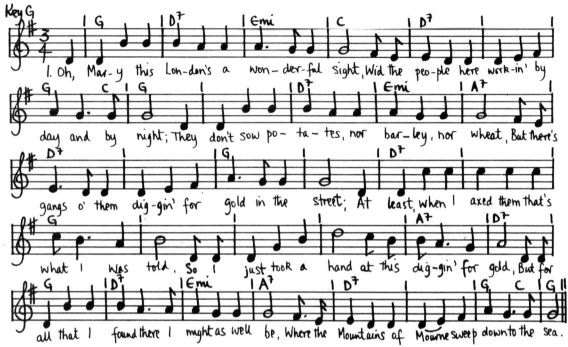

I believe that, when writin', a wish you expressed
As to how the fine ladies in London were dressed.
   Well, if you'll believe me, when axed to a ball,
   They don't wear a top to their dresses at all!
Oh, I've seen them meself, and you could not, in throth,
Say if they were bound for a ball or a bath –
   Don't be startin' them fashions now, Mary Machree,
   Where the Mountains o' Mourne sweep down to the sea.

I seen England's King from the top of a 'bus –
I never knew him, though he means to know us:
   And though by the Saxon we once were oppressed,
   Still, I cheered – God forgive me – I cheered wid the rest.
And now that he's visited Erin's green shore,
We'll be much better friends than we've been heretofore,
   When we've got all we want, we're as quiet as can be
   Where the Mountains o' Mourne sweep down to the sea.

118

You remember young Peter O'Loughlin, of course —
Well, here he is now at the head o' the Force,
　　I met him today, I was crossin' the Strand,
　　And he stopped the whole street wid wan wave of his hand:
And there we stood talking of days that are gone,
While the whole population of London looked on;
　　But for all these great powers, he's wishful like me
　　To be back where dark Mourne sweeps down to the sea.

There's beautiful girls here — oh, never mind!
With beautiful shapes Nature never designed,
　　And lovely complexions, all roses and crame,
　　But O'Loughlin remarked wid regard to them same:
'That if at those roses you venture to sip,
The colour might all come away on your lip,'
　　So I'll wait for the wild rose that's waitin' for me —
　　Where the Mountains o' Mourne sweep down to the sea.

Drumcolliher

Words and music by
PERCY FRENCH

120

They tell me there's Isles of the Ocean
By India's golden shore,
Where life all day long is a beautiful song,
With flowers and fruits galore;
They tell me the sun does be shining,
With never a cloud in the sky —
But when they have done with their clouds and their sun,
Well, I ups and I says, says I —

> *Chorus:*
>
> 'I suppose you've not been to Drumcolliher?
> Ye haven't? Well now I declare.
> You must wait till you've been to Drumcolliher,
> And seen the fine sun we have there,
> There's only one sun in Drumcolliher,
> But then 'tis a glory to see;
> You may talk till you're dumb, but give me ould Drum,
> For Drum is the place for me.'

I was over in London quite lately,
I gave King Edward a call;
Says the butler, 'He's out, he isn't about,
An' I don't see his hat in the hall;
But if you like to look round, sir,
I think you will have to say,
Apartments like these are not what one sees,
In your country every day.'

> *Chorus:*
>
> Ah! Says I, 'Have ye been to Drumçolliher?
> Ye haven't? Well, now I declare,
> You must wait till you've been to Drumcolliher,
> And seen the fine house we have there.
> There's only one house in Drumcolliher,
> For hardware and bacon, and tay.
> If your master would come we would treat him in Drum.
> Ah! Drum is the place for me.'

No More o' yer Golfin' for Me

Words by
PERCY FRENCH

Music by
HOUSTON COLLISSON

I'm an old-fashioned dog to be larnin' new tricks,
But Murphy came round wid two bags full o' sticks,
At hockey you've *one* club, but here you have six,
  And that's a remarkable thing.
Then Murphy drove off the wee ball. Oh! begor!
It rose through the air, till it looked like a star,
The head of my driver'd gone just as far,
  If it hadn't been tied with a string.

Chorus:

Golf! Golf! Carry me off!
Bury me down by the sea.
The drivers may drive,
But dead or alive,
No more o' yer golfin' for me.

122

When I got to the bunker, of clubs I'd just two,
But one was a brass wan, sez I, 'That'll do;
If the ball won't go over, I'll make it go through,'
   So I slashed and I hammered away.
Then Murphy came up, and sez he, 'Ain't it grand!'
Sez I, 'It's a game I don't quite understand.
How much do they give here for shovellin' sand?
   I'd like to get on by the day.'

   Chorus:

   Golf! Golf! Carry me off!
   Bury me down by the sea.
   The lofters may loft,
   Still my sleep shall be soft
   No more o' yer golfin' for me.

While I stood on the green I heard someone cry 'Four!'
I paid no attention – that wasn't my score,
I had done the nine holes in two hundred or more,
   When a ball hit the back of my head.
With Maguire it's always a blow for a blow,
I had just one club left – as I wheeled on my foe,
'Twas a beautiful lady. Begor! 'twas no go.
   'Did you see where the ball fell?' she said.

   Spoken:

   Did I see?
   No! I hadn't *seen* it exactly, but I understood it was
somewhere adjacent.In fact, to the best of my incapacity it was
somewhere contagious.
   I was goin' to pick it up and give it to her, when she said:'Oh!
don't touch it! That's a lovely lie!'
   Of course, when she said that, I saw she knew all about my
broken head, so I told her how I'd laid off to give her a welt
across the face.
   That made us quite friendly at once, so I took her out of the
firing line for a bit and axed her if we could not make a match
of it.
   She said her match was Colonel Bogey!
   Oh, thim soldiers! We ceevilians don't have a chance!

   Chorus:

   Golf! Golf! Carry me off!
   Bury me down by the sea.
   All the wurrld may go
   To 'Old Bogey'! but oh!
   No more o' yer golfin' for me.

On the Road to Ballybay

Words by
PERCY FRENCH

Music by
MOLLY H. FRENCH

Ballybay, Ballybay,
'Twas a dark and winthry day,
But the sun was surely shinin'
On the road to Ballybay.

'Is this the road to fame and wealth?'
Sez I to Miss Magee;
'Ye've got the brains, ye've got the health,'
Sez Mary Anne to me.
'But still I want a comrade
To praise me an' to blame,
An' keep me from the traps that's laid
Upon the road to fame.'

Ballybay, Ballybay,
No man could go astray
With a guide like her beside him
On the road to Ballybay.

'Is this the road to Paradise?'
Sez I to Miss Magee;
'I'm thinkin' that it might be,'
Sez Mary Anne to me.
Oh, I saw the love-light leppin'
In a pair of roguish eyes,
An' I knew we two were steppin'
On the road to Paradise.

Ballybay, Ballybay,
The birds are far away;
But our hearts they sang together,
On the road to Ballybay.

124

The Emigrant Ship

Words and music by
PERCY FRENCH

1. Bright is the sun a-bove me that is shin-ing High are the hopes of those who round me press Why in my heart a-lone this vain re-pin-ing? Why on my cheek the tear of bit-ter-ness? Ah, they are young and when they feel a yearn-ing they may per-chance re-cross the an-gry foam. But to the old, what hope of e'er re-turn-ing Back to the land where stood their fath-er's home Ah— Far, far a-way, where ev-er we may roam Far from the land where stood our fa-ther's home, Fond-ly we gaze a-cross the trou-bled wave, to Ire-land once more.

Room, room for all in the land where we are going,
Bread and to spare, our little ones to feed,
No fear of want, to set dissension growing,
No fear the crops will fail us in our need.
Still whilst around me youthful hearts are sleeping,
Back o'er the wave, my spirit seems to roam,
Once more I see the Shannon by me sweeping,
And the blue mountains of my father's home.
Ah! Far, far away where ever we may roam,
Far from the land where stood our father's home,
Sadly we gaze across the troubled wave, to Ireland once more.

125

The Emigrant's Letter

Words by
PERCY FRENCH

Music by
ERNEST HASTINGS

1. Dear Dan-ny I'm tak-in' the pen in me hand To tell you we're just out o' sight o' the land In the grand Al-lan Li-ner I'm sail-ing in style But I'm sail-ing a-way from the Em-er-ald Isle. And a long sort o' sigh seemed to come from us all As the waves hid the last bit of ould Don-e-gal, Oh, its well to be you that is tak-in' yer tay Where they're cut-tin' the cor-run in Cree-shla the day.

I spoke to the captain – he'll not turn her round,
And if I swam back I'd be apt to be drowned,
So I'll stay where I am and the diet is great
The best of combustibles piled on me plate.
But though it is 'sumpchus', I'd swop the whole lot,
For the ould wooden spoon and the stirabout pot;
And Katie forninst me a-wettin' the tay
Where they're cuttin' the corn in Creeshla the day!

126

There's a woman on board who knows Katey by sight,
So we talked of ould times till they put out the light.
    I'm to meet the good woman tomorra on deck
    And we'll talk about Katey from this to Quebec.
I know I'm no match for her, oh! not the leesht,
Wid her house and two cows and her brother a preesht,
    But the woman declares Katey's heart's on the say,
    While mine's wid the reapers in Creeshla the day.

If Katie is courted by Patsey or Mick,
Put a word in for me with a lump of a stick,
    Don't kill Patsey outright, he has no sort of chance,
    But Mickey's a rogue you might murther at wance;
For Katie might think as the longer she waits
A boy in the hand is worth two in the States:
    And she'll promise to honour, to love and obey
    Some robber that's roamin' round Creeshla the day.

Ah! Good-bye to you Danny, no more's to be said,
And I think the salt wather's got into me head,
    For it drips from me eyes when I call to me mind,
    The friends and the colleen I'm leavin' behind;
But still she might wait; when I bid her goodbye
There was just the laste taste of a tear in her eye,
    And a break in her voice when she said 'You might stay,
    But plaze God you'll come back to ould Creeshla some day.'

Mick's Hotel

Words and music by
PERCY FRENCH

1. Has an-y-bo-dy ev-er been to Mick's Ho-tel, Mick's Ho-tel by the salt say wa-ter? None o' yez ha' been there, just as well! Just as well for ye! Oh! If ye were an os-the-ridge ye might con-trive To get a-way from the place a-live, They charge you a dol-lar for a meal you could-n't swal-ler, And it's down by the sil-ver sea. Oh yes I've been there Yes I was green there Hop-ing that the wait-er might per-haps at-tend to me What's in that tur-een there? "Soup sir, it's been there" Ne-ver a-gain for me —.

You're going in the morning, and you'll want to pay your bill.
Bill! oh, the bill by the salt say water!
If you want to see the size of it you've got to climb a hill,
Or spread it on the silver sea.
They work by 'double entry' – then they multiply by three
And still there's three and sixpence that they haven't got from me.
'Oh, ye washed his flannel collar, put down "laundary" – one dollar
   Though ye washed it in the silver sea.'
Oh yes, I've been there,
Cleaned out quite clean there.
The waiter can't explain the bill, and Mick you never see.
Oh yes, I've been there,
I got quite lean there;
Never again for me.

I went up to the bedroom but I couldn't find the soap,
'Soap! is it soap by the salt say water?'
I went to ring the bell, but I couldn't find the rope,
And the waiter says to me,
'What the divil do ye want with a bedroom bell,
Haven't you a voice, and can't you yell!'
I made the waiter holler! But it cost me a dollar
    Down by the silver sea.
Oh yes, I've been there,
Wits sure are keen there,
But I was in no humour for the lad's jocosity;
Yes, I have been there,
Mick's King and Queen there.
Never again for me.

'You're waiting for your breakfast, sir, and now what will you take?
Fish! is it fish by the salt say water?
All gone up to Dublin, sir, before you were awake.'
'Kidneys and toast and tea.'
'Well, now, there was a kidney, but I think it was last week,
Oh, the tea and the toast isn't far to seek,
And marmalade to folla', that'll cost another dollar,
    Down by the silver sea.'
Oh, I have been there,
Yes, I've been seen there,
Hoping against hope for that second cup of tea.
Oh yes, I've been there,
Shall I be seen there?
Never again for me.

Slattery's Mounted Fut

Words and music by
PERCY FRENCH

1. You've heard of Jul-ius Cae-sar, and of great Na-po-leon too, And how the Cork Mil-i-tia beat the Turks at Wa-ter-loo, But there's a page of glo-ry that, as yet, re-mains un-cut, And that's the war-like sto-ry of the Slat-ter-y Mount-ed Fut. This gal-lant corps was or-gan-ised by Slat-ter-y's eld-est son, A *single mind-ed poach-er with a doub-le-breast-ed gun, And man-ya head was o-pen'd aye, and man-yan eye was shut, While learn-ing to man-oeu-vre in the Slat-ter-y Mount-ed Fut. And down from the mountains came the squad-rons and pla-toons, Four and twen-ty fight-in' men and a cou-ple of stout gos-soons, An' when we marched be-hind the drum to pat-ri-ot-ic tunes, We vowed that fame would gild the name of Slat-ter-y's Light Dra-goons.

*'Noble' is universally used, but daughter Ettie remembers him using the better suited 'single'.

130

Well, first we reconnoithered round o' O'Sullivan's Shebeen –
It used to be 'The Shop House', but we call it 'The Canteen';
But there we saw a notice which the bravest heart un-nerved –
'All liquor must be settled for before the drink is served'.
So on we marched, but soon again each warrior's heart grew pale,
For risin' high in front of us we saw the County Jail;
An' when the army faced about, 'twas just in time to find,
A couple o' policemen had surrounded us behind.

> *Chorus*:
>
> Still down from the mountains came the squadrons and platoons,
> Four-an'-twinty fightin' men, an' a couple o' stout gossoons;
> Says Slattery, 'We must circumvent these bludgeonin' bosthoons,
> Or else it sames they'll take the names o' Slattery's Light Dhragoons.'

'We'll cross the ditch,' our leader cried, 'an' take the foe in flank,'
But yells of consternation here arose from every rank,
For posted high upon a tree we very plainly saw,
'Trespassers prosecuted, in accordance wid the law'.
'We're foiled!' exclaimed bowld Slattery, 'here ends our bowld campaign,
'Tis merely throwin' life away to face that mearin' dhrain,
I'm not as bold as lions, but I'm braver nor a hen,
An' he that fights and runs away will live to fight again.'

> *Chorus*:
>
> An' back to the mountains went the squadrons and platoons,
> Four-an'-twinty fightin' men an' a couple o' stout gossoons;
> The band was playing cautiously their patriotic tunes;
> So sing the fame, if rather lame, o' Slattery's Light Dhragoons.

They reach'd the mountain safely, though all stiff and sore with cramp,
Each took a wet of whisky nate to dissipate the damp,
And when they loaded all their pipes, bowld Slattery ups and said,
'Today's immortal fight will be remembered by the dead:
I never shall forget,' says he, 'while this brave heart shall beat,
The eager way ye followed when I headed the retreat,
Ye preferred the soldier's maxim, when desisting from the strife,
"Best be a coward for five minutes than a dead man all your life".'

> *Chorus*:
>
> An' there in the mountains lay, in squadrons and platoons,
> Four-an'-twinty fightin' men and a couple o' stout gossoons,
> They never more will march again to patriotic tunes;
> Though all the same they sing the fame o' Slattery's Light Dhragoons.

The *Mary Ann McHugh*

Words by
PERCY FRENCH

Music by
PHILIP GREEN

1. Come all ye lads who plough the seas, and like-wise seize the plough— 'Tis the tale of a can-al boat that I'm tell-in' to you now— It was the Ma-ry Ann Mc Hugh that braved the an-gry surf— And bore a-way from Mul-lin-gar with a ter-ri-ble load of turf. And the cap-tain's name was Duff, and his man-ners they were rough. But ev'-ry cape and head-land by it's chris-ti-an name he knew. And he is-sued this com-mand "Keep her well in sight of land 'Till we make the Port of Dub-lin in the Ma-ry Ann Mc Hugh—".

The engine was of one horse-power, propelled wid a blackthorn stick,
With the wind astern, and filled with corn, the horse went a terrible lick.
We worked her roun' the Hill o' Down, and then Kilcock we passed,
And when we seen John Flynn's shebeen, we cried out 'Land at last.'

But the captain, James Duff,
Cried 'Luff! ye lubbers, luff!
   And don't put in near Johnny Flynn whatever else ye do.
Last time we passed his door
We forgot to pay his score,
   So he's got the polis watching for the *Mary Ann McHugh.*'

Then up spoke an old sailor who had sailed the Irish Sea;
'I pray thee put into yonder point or the crew will mutinee;
To put to sea with the boy and me is a cruel thing, I think,
With water, water everywhere, and never a drop o' drink!'

But the captain, Jamesy Duff,
Said 'Enough, my lad, enough!
    No man before the mast shall ever tell me what to do.
Clap on all sail at wance,
For that's our only chance,
    To keep from debt and danger in the *Mary Ann McHugh*.'

With anxious hearts the vessel starts upon her altered course,
The wind and waves they lashed the shore, and the pilot lashed the horse,
But all in vain – beneath the strain the rope began to part,
And she ran aground on a lump of coal that wasn't put down in the chart!

And the captain, Jamesy Duff,
He caught me such a cuff,
    And then he said, 'Go heave the lead,' while the flag at half-mast flew,
But I had had enough
Of the tyrant, Jamesy Duff,
    So I heaved the lead at his head and fled from the *Mary Ann McHugh*.

Rowel Friers

133

Donnegan's Daughter

Words by
PERCY FRENCH

Music by
HOUSTON COLLISSON

She sang the most beautiful songs —
Of the words we had never a hint,
For her fingers went hammer and tongs
In a running accompaniment.
Like a dog running after a rat,
Such scrimmaging never was heard,
Then down went her claws, like a murdering cat
When it leps on the back of a bird.

At every party
She sang them all forte
From 'Ah Ché la morte'
To 'Wearin' the Green'.
 Oh! Donnegan's daughter,
From over the water,
'Twas little they taught her
In Ballyporeen.

The Geraghtys gave a grand dance,
The girls were all ribbons and tapes
But Miss Donnegan gave them no chance
With her perfectly wonderful shapes.
And when she was taking the floor
With a high-stepping bachelor boy,
The rest of us scowled
In the doorway and growled
That 'twas him we would surely destroy.

Chorus:

There was kissing and squeezing
And coaxing and teasing
And sure 'tis no reason
Such things should be seen.
But Donnegan's daughter
From over the water,
'Twas she made the slaughter
In Ballyporeen.

Coming home we were crossing a stream:
I thought to beleaguer the belle;
A struggle, a kiss, and a scream
And into the water we fell.
To me that can swim like a trout
It was only a trifling reverse:
But when she came out,
'Faith there wasn't much doubt
She was changed very much for the worse.

Chorus:

For her roses had wilted,
Her wig it was tilted,
The figure she'd built, it
Was washed away clean:
Oh! Donnegan's daughter
From under the water,
Two pins would have bought her
In Ballyporeen.

POEMS
PARODIES
RECITATIONS
&
SKETCHES

PERCY FRENCH

Ballinaddy

What's to do in Ballinaddy?
    What's the band for did ye say?
The man that killed Jack Donahue
    Is coming home today!
Oh, the boys of Ballinaddy
    May be neither good nor great,
But there's two things we can do here
    We can love, and we can hate!

I should ha' killed the man meself
    Before the girl went wrong,
But then I never thought she'd go
    An' Jack was big and strong;
An' Regan her old sweetheart
    Was the man to interfere
But he was in a sailin' ship
    So how was he to hear?

When Regan came across the say
    To give the girl his name,
When he heard that she was dead,
    And the story of her shame,
He just put down his naggin,
    An' rached out for his hat
Sayin', 'Boys, I must be goin','
    Soft and paceable – like that.

He was back in half an hour,
    An', sez he, 'I cannot tell
If the little girl's in Hivin,
    But Jack Donahue's in Hell!'
They brought it in manslaughter,
    'Killed by an unchancy blow'.
Ah, but there was HATE behind it,
    That the jury didn't know.

Wan year they gave to Regan,
    And now his time is run,
Oh, we've got the bonfires ready,
    From Knocklade to Cushendun,
There's boys from Ballyneety
    An' girls from Ballinthray,
For the man that murthered Donahue
    Is coming home today.

Oh! the boys of Ballinaddy
    Are no credit to the State,
But there's two things we can do here,
    We can love – and we can hate!

When The Winkles Are Asleep

When the winkles are asleep
In their shells beside the deep
With my blue black lady lobster
From the seaweed we will creep.
With my claw around her shell
The old old tale I'll tell
To my little lobster lady
When the winkles are asleep.

Then come, my stalk-eyed Queen,
And a harvest we will glean
Of barnacles and brachipods,
You know the sort I mean.
Far beneath the ebb and flow
O'er the seaweeds we will creep,
Claw in claw we two will wander
While the winkles are asleep.

L'Envoi

Only the seabird now its way may wing
    From crested wave to crest,
And great cloud galleons in the azure swing.
    'After life's battle,' they are murmuring,
    'There shall be rest.'

The End Of The Holiday

Fold up the box, the wind is chill,
    The hills are turning grey,
Tomorrow I must pay my bill,
    And speed me far away –
Back to the world again – but still
    Thank God for such a day!

138

When Erin Wakes

Let newer nations fill the stage,
And vaunt them to the sky:
The Gael has still a heritage
That gold can never buy;
The mountains may be bleak and bare,
Forlorn the countryside,
But great Cuchulainn battled there
And 'Red Branch' heroes died.
And as of old, our headlands bold
Still front the raging sea,
So may our band united stand,
As fearless and as free.

I hear the lays of other days
In martial numbers flow,
King Death's the only sword that stays
The march of Owen Roe.
At Fontenoy the breezes bore
The war cry of the Gael,

And Saxon standards fled before
The sons of Innisfail.
And as of old our headlands bold
Still front the raging sea,
So may our band united stand
As fearless and as free.

Beneath the rath the heroes sleep,
Their steeds beside them stand,
Each falchion from its sheath shall leap
To guard old Ireland:
The legend we may yet fulfil
And play the heroes' part
For Sarsfield's spirit slumbers still
In many an Irish heart.
And as of old our headlands bold
Still front the raging sea,
So may our band united stand
As fearless and as free.

The Kindly Welcome

Ah! 'twill only be a shower,
  Tho' the wind is from the West,
Just come in for half an hour
  And give yerself a rest.

And was that what ye wor sketchin' –
  Just the turf stack an' the whins?
And yer death o' cowld yer ketchin' –
  Mary Ann, put out them hins!

An' that picture, do ye say now
  Ye could sell for thirty bob?
Still, this paintin' in a way now
  Is a very lonesome job.

* * *

Oh! now yer welcome, honey,
  To a little sup like that;
Is it me be takin' money
  For what wouldn't feed the cat!

Only 'Goodnight'

Only 'goodnight' sweetheart,
And not farewell
Though for all time thou art
Where Angels dwell.

Though for a time those eyes
Lose their soft light,
Let there be no goodbyes,
Only goodnight.

Though for a time they toll
Thy passing bell,
'Tis but goodnight, sweet soul,
And not farewell.

O'er thy sweet lips I sigh,
Lips cold and white,
There! – that is not goodbye,
Only 'goodnight'.

That Dividend

'I shall draw about thirty,' McGander remarked,
'And then I shall bolt for the Rhine;
Leave the steamer at Rotterdam, cycle to Bonn,
That is, if the weather be fine.

'You remember last Whitsuntide, all that we missed
Was the price of a dinner at Bray;
But now we are going (the cycle be praised)
To work in a different way.

'I shall push on to Switzerland, visit Lucerne,
And bathe in the Schaffhausen fall;
Coast over the Alps, from Mecredy I learn
The country's not hilly at all.'

'And I,' cried Jack Assleigh, 'I mean to be off,
As soon as my dividend's paid;
Do the Black Forest thoroughly – two days in Prague,
Then make a bee-line for Belgrade.

'My next move I haven't decided upon,
But Russia I think I'll enjoy;
For "The Dnieper, the Dneister, the Volga and Don"
Are names that I loved as a boy.'

'Give me,' cried O'Blither, 'the Lombardy Plain,
And the wonderful city that rears
Its palaces out of the odorous main,
The home of the two gondoliers.

'From Rome on to Athens, the route I shall take
Is one that no scholar should shirk;
Till I land at Scutari, and taking the caïque,
I beard the "Unspeakable Turk".'

They have ordered new cycles, they've ordered new suits,
And though they eat meat other days,
For a week they have simply been living on routes
Which they find in the leaflets of Gaze.

But a letter has come, 'The directors regret
That owing to law and bad trade,
Et cet'ra, et cet'ra, they find they're in debt,
And the dividend cannot be paid.'

They have not been to Bingen, they've not been to Rome,
They've not seen the Maritime Alps;
McGander's at Stepaside, Assleigh's at home,
And O'Blither has been to the Scalp.

Cremorne

When Vauxhall had vanished and Ranelagh's reign
Was ending its glories as fashion's fair fane,
A goddess arose and allegiance was sworn
By Belle and by Beau to my Lady Cremorne.

The worship of Beauty was not thought a crime,
Well, not in that early Victorian time;
Laughter and song on the breezes were borne,
They lived and they loved in the Halls of Cremorne.

They were gay, they were gallant, they lived and died hard,
And fortunes were lost on the turn of a card;
Plucking the roses and planting a thorn,
Playing with love 'neath the lights of Cremorne.

The ladies were careless perhaps, but the men
All guarded their honour most carefully then;
You pushed past a roué, his ruffle was torn,
'Twas pistols for two in a field near Cremorne.

Other times other manners, and Chelsea did well
When she closed the resort of the Beau and the Belle;
The light feet are weary, the gay plumes are shorn
That danced 'neath the lamps of my Lady Cremorne.

Can we sit in judgment? Can anyone say
The follies of London have all passed away?
Sleep, let her sleep, she is weary and worn,
Dust and ashes is all that is left of Cremorne.

Fighting McGuire

Now, Gibbon has told the story of old,
    Of the Fall of the Roman Empire,
But I would recall the rise an' the fall
    Of a man of the name of McGuire,
He came to our town as a man of renown,
    And peace was, he said, his desire,
Still he'd frequently state what would be the sad fate
    Of the man who molested McGuire.

Well, we all were afraid of this quarrelsome blade,
    An' we told him to draw near the fire,
An' laughed at his jest, tho' it wasn't the best,
    An' swore there's no man like McGuire.
An' when he came up with the neighbours to sup,
    His friendliness all would admire,
An' he'd have the best bed – for we'd sleep in the shed
    For fear of insulting McGuire.

But Macgilligan's Dan – who's a rale fightin' man,
    Said, 'Of all this tall talkin' I tire,
I'll step in an' see whyever should he
    Be called always Fightin' McGuire.
I'll step in and say, in a casual way,
    That I think he's a thief an' a liar,
Then I'll hit him a clout, and unless I misdoubt,
    That's a way of insulting McGuire.'

Then onward he strode to McGuire's abode,
    His glorious eye shootin' fire,
An' we thought as he passed we have all looked our last
    On the man who insulted McGuire;
Then we listened with grief while we heard him called thief,
    An' abused as a rogue an' a liar,
Oh! we all held our breath, for we knew it was death
    To give any chat to McGuire.

Well, the row wasn't long, but 'twas hot an' 'twas strong
    An' the noise it grew higher an' higher,
Then it stopt! – an' we said, 'Oh begorra, he's dead!
    He's been kilt out an' out be McGuire!'
Then out like a thrush from a hawthorn bush
    Came something in tattered attire,
And after it fled the man we thought dead –
    The man who malthreated McGuire.

'Twas Macgilligan's son, the victory won,
   An' we crowded around to admire
The bowld-hearted boy who was first to distroy
   The Yoke of the Tyrant McGuire.
An' altho' it's not true, we all said that we knew
   From the first he was only a liar,
An' we'd all had a mind to attack – from behind –
   That cowardly scoundrel – McGuire.

There Was A Little Hen

I

There was a little hen, on some duck eggs she was settin'
An' always kep' forgettin' that the eggs were not her own.
She hatched them out and then
Didn't every son and daughter
Go sailin' on the water,
While she was left alone.

Refrain

'Quack, quack, quack quack quack,'
Went the ducks upon the water.
'Tcahk, tcahk, tcahk tcahk tcahk,'
Went the hen along the shore.
'Oh little ducklin', ducklin', come you back asthore!'
'No!' says the ducklin' chucklin',
'We'll come back no more.'

II

Then up came the chanticleer an' says he, 'What's all the clatter?
Whatever is the matter that you shake in every limb?'
Says she, 'Those eggs of mine
With me have played the dickens.
They're ducks instead of chickens
An' I don't know how to swim.'

Refrain

'Quack, quack, quack quack quack,'
Went the ducks upon the water.
'Tcahk, tcahk, tcahk tcahk tcahk,'
Went the hen along the shore.
'Oh little ducklin', ducklin', come you back asthore!'
'No!' says the ducklin' chucklin',
'We'll come back no more.'

142

The Three Ages Of Man, As Described By Andy Geraghty To His Son

1

'In our lives there's just three ages,'
Said old Andy to his son,
'In the first we're looking forward
To the divilmint and fun,
The divarshin we'll be up to
When our boyhood's days are done:
And we're plannin' and contrivin'
For the years a long time hence,
When we'll play the puck with everything
And spend our father's pence;
That's the age of Happy Childhood –
That's the age of Innocence!

2

'Then we come to the fulfilment
Of the fun for which we schemed,
Which we planned throughout our boyhood
And of which we fondly dreamed.
Though the fruit we taste is never
Quite as pleasant as it seemed,
Still we do our best endeavour
To have a roaring time,
And go in for every divilmint
Just stoppin' short of crime;
That's the age of sense and reason –
That is manhood's glorious prime!

3

'Then the springtime being over,
And the joys of summer past,
When the autumn winds are wailin'
And the skies are overcast,
You will feel the chills of winter
Creeping through your limbs at last;
Then recallin' the divarshins,
The divilmint and fun,
You think about repentin'
Of the evil you have done;
That, my son, is called your Dotage,
When your mind is nearly gone.'

To E. R.

(E. R. was a fellow guest at Glenveigh Castle who 'fancied' their hostess)

For you once heard the fairy bells,
　　And saw the little shehogues play,
And knew at last the magic spells
　　That lead the lover to Glenveigh.

Oh Poet, when the touch of Time
　　Has turned those auburn locks to grey,
Still may the Bells of Faerie chime,
　　That once re-echoed round Glenveigh.

The Next Landing Of The French

Oh! the French is on the say,
　　Says the Shan Van Voght,
He'll be here widout delay,
　　Says the Shan Van Voght.
He's been gone for many a day,
By them Saxons led asthray,
Och, sure them's the boys can pay!
　　Says the Shan Van Voght.
He has all his latest jokes,
　　Says the Shan Van Voght.
And he draws wid lightning strokes,
　　Says the Shan Van Voght.
And that song wid quaint refrain,
Of 'The Clare Excursion Train',

You will want to hear again
　　Says the Shan Van Voght.
How should Irish songs be sung?
　　Says the Shan Van Voght.
Will he try the ancient tongue?
　　Says the Shan Van Voght.
Oh! the Irish may be grand
But the tongue at his command
Is the one we understand,
　　Says the Shan Van Voght.
Tho' the Green Isle of the West
May have brought him many a jest,
'Tis the land he loves the best!
　　Says the Shan Van Voght.

Later On

When we're children at our lessons, it is beautiful to think
    Of the good time that is coming later on;
When we've done with silly copybooks and horrid pens and ink,
    What a lovely time is coming later on!
The rivers of New Zealand, the mountains of Peru,
The watersheds of Europe, and the tribes of Timbuctoo,
All the facts without the fancies, all the tiresome and true,
    Will be nowhere in that lovely later on.

We'll forget the foolish fables that were written by Fontaine,
    In the pleasant time that's coming later on;
At those twelve times twenty tables we will never look again,
    In the lazy time that's coming later on.
The date of Magna Charta, the plot they called 'the Rye',
The counties that are bounded by the Humber and the Wye,
We may not quite forget them, but we mean to have a try,
    In the lazy time that's coming later on.

Oh, my optimistic hero, there are lessons you must learn
    In the queer time that is coming later on;
And masters and examiners you'll find at every turn,
    In the hard times that are coming later on.
Miss Fortune is a governess who'll teach you many things,
A tutor called Experience will moderate your flings,
You'll learn how men make money, and you'll learn that it has wings
    In the strange times that are coming later on.

Then you'll meet the radiant vision who is all the world to you
    (You'll attend her mother's lectures later on);
You'll learn that what's enough for one is not enough for two,
    Nor enough for half-a-dozen later on.
No, the work is never ended, though for holidays you crave,
There are pop-guns to be mended for the Robbers in the Cave.
You fancy you're the master, but you find that you're a slave
    To a curly-headed tyrant later on.

And so through all your lifetime you are longing for the day,
    The lovely day that's coming later on;
When pens and ink and copybooks will all be laid away,
    And that day is surely coming later on.

For when you're really tired, having done your level best,
When the story's nearly ended, and the sun sets in the West,
Then you'll lie down very gently, and the weary will find rest,
    And I fancy we'll deserve it – later on.

144

Later on, later on,
Oh the many friends have gone,
Sweet lips that smiled and loving eyes that shone.
Through the darkness into light,
One by one they've winged their flight
And perhaps we'll play together – later on.

A Comic Advertisement

The Painter and the Pianist
  Were walking hand-in-hand,
'Suppose we try,' the Painter said,
  'To give a one night stand,
With me to write the dialogue,
  And you to be the band!'

'Suppose we gave six Matinées,'
  Replied the Pianist,
'And cater for the young and old
  In ways they can't resist.'
'Do you suppose,' the Painter said,
  'That we should both be hissed?'

'I doubt it,' said the Pianist,
  'I've always got recalls,
And you have got a pretty wit,
  A wit that never palls.'
'We'll give a week,' the Painter said,
  'In Steinway's pillared Halls.'

Now don't forget on Boxing Day,
  From three to nearly five,
For just a week this merry pair
  Will keep the game alive;
So on that day jump on a 'bus
  And tell it where to drive.

And if the driver says he's got
  To go to London Wall,
Or Parsons Green or Shepherd's Bush,
  You answer, 'Not at all,
The only place that people go
  This week is – Steinway Hall!'

Song Of William, Inspector Of Drains

Let others betake them to Western Plains
And ease the redman of his ill-gotten gains;
No tomahawk ever shall injure the brains
Of William, the Local Inspector of Drains.

He mounts his tall trap, gives his charger the reins,
And gallops away through the green country lanes,
The Board pays the posting – the balance remains –
With William, the Local Inspector of Drains.

He finds out the holding and what it contains,
Then maps out his system in furlongs and chains,
And points out positions for 'miners' and 'mains' –
Such wisdom has William, Inspector of Drains.

He plunges through marshes long haunted by cranes,
Unmindful of how the dark bog-water stains;
Traducers assert that this ardour he feigns,
They little know William, Inspector of Drains!

He stays in his quarters, of course, if it rains,
And wakes the piano's voluptuous strains,
And if of delay the bold tenant complains,
He's sat on by William, Inspector of Drains.

The fair maids of Cavan (this William maintains,
Tho' I think one should take it with salt, a few grains)
Have left in a body their woe-begone swains
For William, the Local Inspector of Drains!

'Tis an onerous post – but the writer refrains
From dwelling at length on its pleasures and pains,
It may not last long, but as yet he remains
        Yours faithfully,
          (William)
          Inspector of Drains.

Mr Parnell At Thurles

Oh, man, did they poison your skilly,
Or give you some hypnotized toke,
That you've broken your word to me, Willy,
And fled to the Sassenach yoke?
To traducers I've always responded,
He's brave and as bold as a line
And true to the core – and beyond it!
Is William O'Brine.

I had a sweet message to send him,
Our friendship I hoped to restore;
But now he's away – Divil mend him!
Mayhap I shall meet him no more,
And Dillon I asked to the Gresham,
I ordered a bottle of wine
(And two kinds of cake) to refresh him
And William O'Brine.

My friendship for him was a strong one,
He sent me his novel to read;
I read it (although it's a long one)
And live to remember the deed.
I told him the plot was intricate,
I told him the writing was fine,
I didn't think perjury wicked
When pleasing O'Brine.

I wasn't quite sure about Dillon;
Though when he was over the wave
He seemed to be perfectly willun
To trust in my power to save;
And even before his arrest, too,
He told me he meant to combine,
And stick to his old manifesto
With William O'Brine.

O Timpora! also O Mores!
Does any one happen to know
Am I treating with Whigs or with Tories,
And which of me friends is me foe?
Whether Liberal back me or Tory
No matter I'll never resign;
But right to the end of the story,
In spite of O'Brine!

Celestial Painting
Sunset at Renvyle

When painters leave this world, we grieve
   For the hand that will work no more,
But who can say that they rest alway
   On that still celestial shore?

No! No! they choose from the rainbow hues,
   And winging from Paradise,
They come to paint, now bold, now faint,
   The tones of our sunset skies.

When I see them there I can almost swear
   That grey is from Whistler's brain!
That crimson flush was Turner's brush!
   And the gold is Claude Lorraine.

People I Don't Want To Meet

There are people who say
It is wrong to be gay
In this workaday world of ours;
   They live far apart
   From the pleasures of art
Discarding the sweets for the sours.
   One would think from their creeds
   God gave us the weeds,
And the Devil provided the flowers.

   Of course I'm aware,
   Earthly joys are a snare,
And the laugh from my lips I should banish;
   I ought to throw dust
   On my head – but I must
Catch that silvery gleam ere it vanish.
   As my colours combine,
   What a kingdom is mine!
Though most of my castles are Spanish.

Rafting Down The Rio

Come sit beside the fire, old friend,
 And dream that bamboo stems
Have risen up around us
 'Mid flowers that shine like gems,
And we are back in fairyland,
 And thro' the golden haze
We're rafting down the Rio –
 In the old Jamaica days.

Oh! the old Jamaica days!
 Faintly through that leafy maze
Comes the croon of Creole melodies
 As down the stream one strays;
Till the fireflies sparkle round us
 In those darkened waterways,
And we're rafting down the Rio –
 In the old Jamaica days.

In those mighty mountain ranges
 What memories lie hid,
Through the stricken streets of Kingston
 Stalks the ghost of Captain Kidd.
While a phantom Henry Morgan
 Sets Port Royal in a blaze,
As we're rafting down the Rio –
 In the old Jamaica days.

Oh! the old Jamaica days!
 How we used to lie and laze,
And think of people working
 As a curious kind of craze;
Wear and tear of brain and muscle
 How we wondered if it pays,
As we rafted down the Rio –
 In the old Jamaica days.

There's a terror in the tree tops,
 And where the shadows brood,
For the wild cat and the scorpion
 And the snakes are seeking food.
The alligators blink at us,
 From fever-haunted bays,
And the woods knew Devil worship –
 In those old Jamaica days.

Oh! the old Jamaica days!
 When the sun's mid-winter rays
Have failed to pierce the fogs that fill
 Our murky alleyways
We'll sit beside the fire, old friend,
 And as the embers blaze,
Go rafting down the Rio –
 In the old Jamaica days.

Lines In A Swiss Hotel (any of them)

There's German in the music room
 There's French upon the stair,
There's English in the Grand Salon,
 There's laughter everywhere.
A bunch from Boston hold their own
 At every sort of noise,
O Switzerland! O Switzerland!
 The land for healthy boys!

'We're off to bob,' 'We're off to ski,'
 'We'll not be home till late.'
'A curling match? – well, after tea –
 This morning I must skate.'
'Our trailing party starts at ten!'
 And off to sport one whirls,
O Switzerland! O Switzerland!
 The land for growing girls!

In leafy dells love weaves his spells
 Where southern sunsets glow,
And hand in hand thro' fairyland
 The lovers wander slow.
But hearts can throb on board a 'bob',
 We want no woodland glades,
O Switzerland! O Switzerland!
 The land for men and maids.

Some day, old friend, I'd love to take
 Our families and go
From London to Lucerne – and walk
 Amid the sun and snow,
And see ourselves in joyous elves,
 (Our daughters and our sons),
O Switzerland! O Switzerland!
 The land for weary ones!

The Musician To His Love

Sing me no song! Give me one silent hour!
   Your nerve is strong, but mine's a fragile flower;
Sing when I'm far from here, say in Hong Kong;
   But, if you love me, dear, sing me no song.

When I the prelude played, and bade you sing,
   Oh! the strange noise we made! The jangling!
White notes I found were wrong, so were the black!
   For you had pitched the song right in the crack!

If you were dumb, and not a single note
   Could ever come from out that rounded throat,
Songs you might spell on finger and on thumb,
   Oh, I could love you well if you were dumb!

If I were deaf, oh! then I'd let you sing
   In C or F, and watch the guests take wing;
I'd let thee shriek and yell above the treble clef,
   That would not break the spell – if I were deaf!

You have no ear – no ear for tune or rhyme,
   And, it is very clear, no sense of time.
Sing to my wealthy aunt, her nerves are strong,
   But, if it's me you want – sing me no song!

Off To The West Indies

Dear ones in my happy home
We are sailing o'er the foam
Anchor tripped and helm a-lee
(Not quite sure what that may be)
For the Caribbean Sea!

Doctor looking rather pale
Prospect of a six-days' sail!
Only fancy, we shall glide,
Where the wild Bahamas ride.

What they ride I never knew,
Will know it in a day or two –
Live on flying fish and fruits,
Empty scorpions from our boots!

Mounted on a trusty steed,
Chase the deadly centipede,
Beard the beetle in his den,
'On a peak of Darien'.

Then with faces wreathed in smiles
Turning from the Windward Isles,
Sail across the wobbling main
Till we reach our homes again.

The Wreck Of The *Michael Connor*

They cheered to see our canvas fill,
And passed the time o' day,
Shore-going swabs from Misery Hill
And boys from Charlotte Quay.

'Bring us a monkey home,' they cried,
'Bring us a parrowket,'
And the captain deep in his beard replied,
'I'll bring yees a weltin' yet.'

Beyond the mountain's purple brow
The sun is sinking down,
When shone upon our Starboard bow
The lights of Irishtown.

The Glass Works we had almost won,
When hark! a sudden thud,
The *Michael Connor's* race is run,
We're grounded in the mud!

'Ho! man the pump, you moochin' chump,'
High rose the pilot's hail,
'And heave the lead at the horse's head,
And beat him abaft the tail.'

In vain, in vain they chuck the rein,
And whack the straining flank,
In sight of land on either hand
The grand old gabber sank.

Mid pots and pans of a bygone time
The foundered vessel lies,
Along its sides the wavelets chime,
Or the seabird slowly flies.

And bearded men from Charlotte's Quay
Still sit on the grassy ridge,
And tell how the good ship sailed away
And sank off Ringsend Bridge.

148

Galloping Hogan
An incident in the Siege of Limerick

'They have sent for fresh artillery,
   The guns are on their way,
God help our hapless Limerick
   When dawns another day.'
Thus speaks the gallant Sarsfield,
   As sadly he recalls
The famine and despair that lurk
   Behind those crumbling walls.

'And yet one blow for freedom –
   One daring midnight ride!
And William may be humbled yet,
   For all his power and pride!
Go! Bring to me "The Galloper",
   To Highway Hogan say
'Tis Ireland has need of him,
   And him alone today!'

The Soldier and the Highwayman
   Are standing face to face,
The fearless front, the eagle eye,
   In both of them we trace.
'Hogan! the night is dark and drear,
   Say, canst thou lead the way
To Keeper Mountain's black ravines
   Ere dawn another day?'

'Can the eagle find his eyrie?
   Can the fox forget his den?
I can lead ye as none other
   Of the Slievecamatha men.
The black mare knows it blindfold,
   It's not by the stars she'll steer,
Ye'll be tonight on the Keeper's height –
   And dawn will find ye here.'

'Lead on!' and well he led them,
   Though the Shannon ford ran deep,
And though the white-lipped flood ran fierce
   Around O'Brien's Keep.
The sentinel on Killaloe
   Looked out, but failed to see –
Five hundred silent horsemen ride
   Behind the Rapparee.

That night by Balleneety's towers
   The English gunners lay.
'King William's Camp and safety lies
   But twelve short miles away.
What need of further caution?
   What Irish wolf would dare
To prowl around our camp tonight,
   So near the lion's lair?'

An Irish wolf is near them now,
   And Irish ears have heard
The chosen watchword for the night,
   And 'Sarsfield' was the word.
A tramp of horse – 'Who's there? The word!'
   'Sarsfield!' the answer ran,
And then the sword smote downwards,
   'Ay, and Sarsfield is the man!'

'To arms! the foe!' Too late, too late,
   Though Villiers' vengeful blade
Is wet with Hogan's life blood,
   As he leads the ambuscade.
Then foot to foot, and hand to hand,
   They battle round the guns,
Till victory declares itself
   For Erin's daring sons.

'Oh for those guns in Limerick now
   Placed on the city walls!
We'd bid King William breakfast
   On his own black cannon balls!
It may not be – but trebly charged,
   And filled with shot and shell,
They'll toll the robber's requiem,
   And sound the soldier's knell,'

Oh, sudden flash of blinding light!
   Oh, hollow-sounding roar!
Down history's page in Irish ears
   It echoes evermore.
And Balleneety's blackened tower
   Still marks the famous place
Where Sarsfield staked his all to win,
   And won that midnight race!

Smiles

When the cat has finished breakfast,
And is sitting by the fire,
The cat that all the tabby cats
Persistently admire,
When that most unpleasant animal,
The dog, is out of doors,
And pussy thinks of how last night
He settled some old scores,
When he thinks about the big black cat
He knocked right off the tiles –
            – He smiles.

When the summer girl has got her frocks,
And this year's set of curls,
When she finds that she's the loveliest
Among a crowd of girls,
When the first unwary masculine
Has met her downcast eye,
When he cannot see the other girls
As long as she is nigh,
When she ascertains there's not another
Man for miles and miles,
            She smiles.

When the German Jew financier
Has bought before the jump,
Manipulates the market,
And unloads before the slump,
When he's harvesting his dollars,
And he finds a goodly crop,
When his friends are at the bottom
And Herr Grabstein's at the top,
When he thinks of all those poor young men
Who did not make their piles,
            He smiles.

When Michael meets wid Mary,
At the back o' the boreen,
An' says, 'Ye've stole me heart away
Ye murtherin' shlieveen,'
When she tells him to give over,
'Can't ye leave a girl alone,'
He crams his hat down on his eyes,
His heart sinks like a stone –
When she takes him home the longest road,
And sits on all the stiles,
            He smiles.

When gesticulating Frenchmen
Tell the masher about France,
How he must see la belle Paree
Whenever he's ze chance,
When Italians talk of Roma,
And the Spaniards talk of Spain,
The Piccadilly Johnny wears
A look of mild disdain –
When they say that there are other towns
Outside the British Isles,
            He smiles.

When Jack has met wi' Janet
By the burn ahint the brae,
Ye dinna ken where yon is?
For mysen I canna say.
When the merlas are foorhooing,
An' the beasties in the byre,
There's something in the lassie's een
That sets his heart on fire.
When he says, 'I'm no unwillin'
If ye would be marrit whiles,'
            She smiles.

When the Yankee tells the British Peer
That in the Empire State
In Washington and Boston
They have culture just as great;
They haven't Will P. Shakespeare,
Or J. Milton in their show,
But they've Field, and Whitcomb Riley,
And they've Harriet Beecher Stowe –
He doesn't contradict them,
Oh, no, he never riles.
            He smiles.

When the farmer's man on Sunday
Gets a 'aircut and a shave,
When he meets wi' Doll the dairy maid,
And she says, 'Do behave'
When he says, 'I've got two pound a week,
I've 'ad another rise,'
Her fortune is her golden hair
And pair of diamond eyes;
So when she hangs around his neck
And sez, 'I love 'e Giles,'
            He smiles.

Etiquette

Sir Diagnosis Stethescope Parietal De Brown
Was perhaps the most astute of all the Medicos in town
But through all his course of study and his practice he would let
No sentiment divert him from his code of Etiquette.

One morning in the hospital a friend he chanced to see
Being treated for insomnia by old Max Hillary
He saw that Max was treating him most ignorantly – yet
He couldn't interfere, of course it wasn't Etiquette.

The days went on – the case grew worse, the nurses in the ward
Had doubts about the treatment, but of course their tongues were barred.
De Brown had thoughts of poisoning Max Hillary and yet
A dose of prussic acid would be hardly Etiquette.

He vowed 'no patient could survive beneath that Upas tree'
'Twas thus that he referred to old Max Hillary, M.D.
His fingers fairly itched to try his hypodermic jet
But couldn't well suggest it as it wasn't Etiquette.

'I fancy,' said Max Hillary, 'some pressure on the brain
I shall find at the Autopsy and be able to explain.'
So all De Brown could do was go with feelings of regret
And drop a tear upon the bier – but that was Etiquette.

The Songs Of A Nation

Dig deep in the earth for thy treasure,
Let ingot on ingot be flung,
But where is the gold that can measure
The worth of the songs we have sung?

Songs of the follies of fashion,
Songs of our labour and rest,
Songs that appeal to the passion
That lies in the love-laden breast.

Songs that have brought consolation
To watchers alone with their dead,
Songs that have maddened a nation
Till tyranny heard them and fled.

With never a sound of the hammer,
With never a stroke of the spade,
With moonlight and starlight and glamour
The songs of the singer are made.

Tell Me, O Captain

'Tell me, O Captain come up from the sea,
   Is there no news from the little green island,
Is there a woman there waiting for me,
   Calling me back to the land that is my land?'

'A woman there was, but 'tis weary she grew,
   Weary of waiting and weary of weeping,
Why do you blame her not waiting for you,
   You with your soul set on sowing and reaping?'

'I thought she'd be true to the word that she said,
   I saw the salt tears in her eyes when she said it,
One more good year and my fortune was made,
   Tell me, O Captain, who was it she wedded?'

'Death was the suitor she had to obey,
   He's laid her to rest in a grave in Glasnevin;
She whispered your name, then they bore her away,
   Go on with your harvest – she's happy in heaven.'

151

She Was Seven

A little maid, a cheeky thing,
Who takes her elders off;
With arms that scarce a club can swing
What can she know of golf?

And such a one I chanced to meet
As I with Bogey played;
It struck me I'd be sure to beat
So young a little maid.

'I'm three holes up, my little maid,
My score is now eleven.'
The little lass looked up and said,
'Good sir, I'm only seven.'

'Seven!' I cried, 'and this your third,
You'll think me an old fogey –
It's marvellous! upon my word,
My dear! you've beaten Bogey!'

'You must have made the first in two;
In two you made your second.
I don't know who's the King, but you
The Golf Queen must be reckoned.'

'Oh, no,' she said, 'I topped the ball
When I was driving off, sir;
And twice I didn't hit at all:
I'm not the Queen of Golf, sir.'

'You foozled every drive,' I cried;
'You now must be eleven!'
'Oh, no!' the little maid replied,
'I only counted seven.'

With gravity, I gazed upon
This most mendacious younker.
'You must have done the next in one!
And so escaped the bunker?'

'Oh, no,' she said, 'I lamned the sand
Until I thought t'would blind me,
Then took the ball up in my hand
And dropped it just behind me.'

'You say you in the bunker stayed?
Why, then, good gracious Heaven!
You must be seventeen,' I said;
'Oh, no,' she said, 'I'm seven.'

'You see, I'm not like other folks;
I may get into messes,
But then I only score the strokes
That I would call successes.'

I placed the brassey to my brow –
My word was not a blest one –
And then I said, 'Sweet maid, I vow
Your method is the best one.'

And all thro' life we would have less
To baffle and to blind us,
If we could only count success
And leave mistakes behind us.

Twas long ago – she's grown up now,
We both are ancient fogies –
But she it is who shows me how
To beat a lot of Bogies.

A Little Girl's Prayer

'Dear Lord – Aunt Jane is good I know
    But then her smiles are scanty,
I do want to be good – but oh!
    Not quite so good as Aunty;
I know that I am understood
    So no more for the present,
P.S. – Make all bad people good
    And all good people – pleasant.'

Tennis

In the world's great game of tennis
Which from pole to pole is seen
Let love be the point of starting,
Faults be few and far between;
Raise no wild unseemly racket,
From base lines of life break loose,
Win no underhand advantage;
This the moral we deduce.

'Gyp'

'Friend of the family' run over and killed by a taxi
14 September, 1912.

I've chanted in praise of the automobile,
For rhymes I have cudgelled my brain,
To sing of the pleasures of touring a-wheel
(Impelled by the prospect of gain).

But now, oh mine editor, let me reverse
My trained intellectual gear,
And just for a season I'll sit down and curse
All motors – the far and the near!

Oh Gyp, little Gyp, he was only a dog
Of no very notable kind,
But I feel as if someone had fastened a log
Round what I consider my mind.

When I think how to greet me a bee-line he made;
But ere the two comrades could meet,
A taxi-cab whizzed round the corner and laid
A crushed little form at my feet.

The back garden blooms in its summer array,
The chestnut trees flame overhead,
His funeral torches we call them today,
While digging his last little bed.

The sparrows no longer need fly for their lives,
The cats in the sunshine lie still,
For only the spirit of Gyppy survives,
To hunt up and down Clifton Hill.

The 'buses may clang and the taxis may scream,
The traffic roll on as of yore,
But Gyppy will never awake from his dream,
And Loudon Road knows him no more.

And still people say that there will come a day
When all our old comrades we'll greet –
Till that merry young pup of a mongrel turns up
My happiness won't be complete!

I would I could send you a merrier stave,
But cars for a time I detest,
My little brown brother lies low in his grave,
So Editor – give me a rest.

A Fairy Song

Stay, silver ray,
Till our airy way we wing
To the shade of the glade
Where the fairies dance and sing:
The mortals are asleep –
They can never understand
That night brings delight,
It is day in Fairyland.

Float, golden note,
From the lute strings all in tune,
Climb, quiv'ring chime,
Up the moonbeams to the moon.
There is music on the river,
There is music on the strand,
Night brings delight,
It is day in Fairyland.

Sing while we swing
From the bluebell's lofty crest.
'Hey! Come and play,
Sleepy songbirds in your nest;
The glow-worm lamps are lit,
Come and join our Elfin band,
Night brings delight,
It is day in Fairyland.'

Roam thro' the home
Where the little children sleep,
Light in our flight
Where the curly ringlets peep.
Some shining eyes may see us,
But the babies understand,
Night brings delight,
It is day in Fairyland.

153

The Valley Of Dunloe

Have the fairies all departed
And left me broken-hearted
To mourn the little creatures we loved so long ago?
Ah! most of them have vanished,
But there's one that isn't banished
For I met her as I wandered in the Valley of Dunloe.

I had stopped awhile to render
In its glory all the splendour
Of the great sun slowly rising, and the morning mists aglow,
And the rocks that rose before me,
And the tree tops bending o'er me,
Standing black against the sunshine that was sweeping down Dunloe.

I put in trees and grasses,
And the summer cloud that passes,
O'er the mountain and its shadow in the valley far below,
But what chalk could tell the story,
The glamour and the glory,
When those golden gleams had flooded all the Valley of Dunloe.

My attempt at shade and colour
Grew dirtier and duller
When compared with radiant nature, and I felt inclined to go —
And bury my endeavour
In the crystal stream for ever,
When I heard a gentle voice say, ''Tis a picture of Dunloe.'

I turned, and lo! a maiden
With a market basket laden
Was watching my endeavour with her bright face all aglow,
I knew she was a fairy
Though she said her name was Mary,
And her father was a farmer in the Valley of Dunloe.

I asked her if she'd let me
Take her portrait, but she met me
With a shake of raven tresses which I knew she meant for 'no'.
Still in spite of her decision
I can draw with some precision
The maid who met my vision in the Valley of Dunloe.

And now when e'er I render
That valley in its splendour
I see a form that's slender and a face with eyes aglow,
And instead of drawing airy
Heights, I find I've drawn sweet Mary
As she stood that summer morning in the Valley of Dunloe.

154

George Grossmith
Died March, 1912

Lay down the pipe and the tabor,
  Set the bell tolling instead,
He is resting at last from his labour
  George Grossmith is dead!

The mirth and the melody blended,
  The laughter that ran with it all!
Ring down the curtain – 'tis ended,
  The player can take no recall.

'Twas first as an actor we found you
  Filling the little Savoy
The Prince of the Jesters we crowned you –
  And wasn't your 'Koko' a joy!

I see you First Lord on the ocean,
  Surrounded by beautiful belles;
I can see you concocting a potion
  As 'Mr John Wellington Wells'.

I can see you as Bunthorne sounding
  The deeps of aesthetic despair;
I can see you when pirates were hounding
  You home to their poisonous lair.

But though you were quite the Top-liner,
  As many a playbill has shown;
To me you were funnier – finer,
  When 'Piano and I' were alone.

How my neighbour would dig all my ribs in,
  And bellow 'Bravo!' and 'Encore!'
When you acted that skit upon Ibsen,
  Or sang of 'The babe on the shore.'

From everything laughter extracting,
  What millions you've made to rejoice
At the biograph's views on your acting,
  The gramophone's gibes at your voice.

The lady and gentleman shopping –
  Irascible folk in the train –
The dentist who finds he's been stopping
  The tooth that had never a pain!

I have laughed at them times without number,
  I know I could laugh at them still;
But the bright brain is dulled in Death's slumber,
  The stage is for others to fill.

And who is there now of us mummers,
  To take up the mantle you threw;
Ten minutes we give the new comers
  – We spent the whole evening with you.

Farewell! my old friend, when we find you
  In garments celestial clad,
We will gather around and remind you
  Of all the gay laughs we have had.

I can fancy the harps ringing sweeter,
  – Can fancy the cherubims' glee,
Can picture the smile of St Peter,
  When welcoming good old G.G.

Farewell! you were ever the one light
  That beamed like a beacon ahead;
– Ah me! there's a chill in the sunlight,
  George Grossmith is dead!

In The Studio

Once more I paint from memory
  The hills of Donegal,
And as they rise – ma Gramachree!
  In fancy I recall
The fairy song you sang for me
  Beside the waterfall.

And when I paint the sparkling tide
  That flows by Slievenaree,
I would the boat again might glide
  Across the summer sea,
And bring the fairy to my side
  Who sang that song for me.

The Fisherman's Wife

When the dusky veil of the night is torn
   When clouds unfold and flee,
When song birds wake, and a saffron morn
   Steals over a silver sea.

Then the bark that she loves is spreading its wings
   To speed on its way again,
And she hears the song that her sailor sings
   As he hauls on the anchor chain.

Alone she stands on the sunlit sands
   And watches the rising sail,
And a clear call floats to the speeding boats
   As she echoes his parting hail.

With anxious eyes she scans the skies
   As the boats glide on and on –
Till over the brink of the ocean they sink
   And the bark that she loves is gone.
And standing there, a little prayer
   Flies after them over the foam,
And she turns away to the toil that day
   Must bring to her cottage home.

And the wavelets fall on the old sea wall
   And beat on the cold grey stones,
Singing the song they have sung so long
   In their musical monotones.
And now and again a low sweet strain
   Floats up to the cliffs above,
For the eyes are bright and the heart is light
   When we work for the one we love.

There's a glow in the West, and it tells that rest
   From the toils of the day is nigh,
And the great sun flings forth its golden wings
   Ere bidding the world good-bye.

Down the golden ways of the sun's last rays
   He comes to her over the foam,
And hand clasps hand on the dark'ning strand
   When the bark that she loves comes home.

The 'Funny Man' At Home

I cannot fill the air with squeals,
I wouldn't if I could;
And if I jumped just after meals,
'Twould do me little good.

But rest awhile on Daddy's knee,
And hide that rosy face,
Upon his breast, and learn that he
In nature has a place.

I have to go and look for gold,
For gold's a sort of charm,
That keeps the lambs within the fold
From every sort of harm.

You do not hear the wolves that creep
Around our home at night,
They only come when you're asleep
And nurse puts out the light.

Red eyes glare at me through the bars,
I know for whom they seek;
It takes two feet of comic 'pars'
To slay them every week.

So if I'm dull and distant at
The game of 'Jumpy Frog',
If I am surly with the cat,
Or seem to snub the dog,

Or if at 'Thumpy' you perceive
A cold and languid tone,
Remember, little one, that we've
Got worries of our own.

156

The Cruise Of The Pirate 'Bus

Sez Bill to me, 'I'm beat,' sez he, 'I haven't a coin to clink,
I can't make both ends meet,' sez he – 'I can't make one end
  drink!'
Sez I to Bill, 'There's a trump card still that hasn't been played
  by us.
We're both mechanics of nerve and skill, let's capture a motor
  'bus.'
We stole her that night; she was green and white, so we painted
  her red and blue,
And you couldn't tell where she had come from, I'll swear, or
  where she was going to.
For we painted names on her hull–'St James', and
  'Richmond', and 'Regent's Park',
'Victoria', too, and 'Waterloo', and 'Kew', by way of a lark!

'Twas merry, 'twas merry in Oxford Street, and we made the
  taxis stare
As we bowled along to Bill's old sea song, 'Hi! tuppence to
  everywhere!'
And we piled them in, then Bill would grin at their looks of hate
  and rage,
When I turned the 'bus round and the passengers found we had
  come to the end of our stage!
We were doing first rate when we shipped a freight of
  gardeners bound for Kew,
And my messmate said, 'There's breakers ahead,' when we
  headed for Waterloo.
To save any fuss I beached the 'bus on an island in the Strand,
Oh! their cries of despair as we left them there, marooned
  within sight o' land!

With a fiendish shout I warped her out, what were their woes to
  us?
Then we shipped a fresh crew and the red flag flew once more
  from the Pirate 'Bus!
By night we'd rest in a mews out west, and there securely hid,
Our coppers we'd count till the total amount was close on a
  hundred quid!
Then a big fog come, and we drove her home to where we had
  found her fust,
And I went to propose to 'The Kilburn Rose', while Bill he went
  on a bust.
A crime? – No doubt, if we'd been found out, we might ha'
  been jugged for life.
But I told this tale by the moonlight pale – and that's how I won
  my wife!

A Reaction

I want to find some place on earth
  Where motors are unknown,
Where hydroplane ne'er skims the main,
  Nor aeroplane's been flown.
High on some heather mountain,
  Beside some hidden stream,
From noise and speed for ever freed,
  I'll lay me down and dream.

I'll dream I hear the reapers as they sing among the sheaves,
And the woodquest softly cooing 'mid the rustling of the leaves,
The wind among the rushes, the rippling of the stream,
Will come to me again and be the burthen of my dream.

When all the world on hydroplanes
  Is rushing through the waves,
And sirens wake the echoes
  Of the seals' remotest caves.
When men rise off the waters
  And go whizzing through the air,
Till the frigate bird who followed them
  Gives up in sheer despair.

I'll dream of summer mornings when the day had just begun,
And the ships went slowly sailing up the pathway of the sun,
And the mellow tops'l chanty came floating back to me
From those dear old 'water bruisers' as they drifted out to sea.

When all the world is flying past
  In bi- and monoplanes,
And not a region unexplored
  From pole to pole remains.
When they're whizzing past our windows,
  And round our chimney pots,
And raining oil and petrol on
  Our little garden plots.

I'll dream of peaceful evenings when the crows came slowly home,
And the bumble bees sang harmonies around the honeycomb.
When the flittermice flew silently along the forest glade,
And from the vale the nightingale sighed forth its serenade.

And now to find that hallowed spot afar from human ken,
Where, haply, motor cars are not, nor aeroplaning men.
And there upon that distant hill, while stars their watches keep,
I'll dream the earth is standing still and everyone's asleep.

158

Lines Written In Praise Of Joan Phyllis French

A young lady, who by constantly disregarding my advice and eating more than was good for her has attained her eleventh year.

I
Oh! Joan, when first you saw the light you
    Caused us much annoy,
For both your parents though you might as well
    Have been a Boy.

II
We *had* two daughters, each a gem – so thought –
    Oh! was it strange?
We'd had about enough of them
    A Boy would be a change.

III
But after standing you for ten long years of
    Peace and War
If you were to be born again we'd want you –
    – As you *are*.

                           Daddy

Not Lost But Gone Before

Once, only once, upon a time,
We heard the bells of faerie chime,
    And through the golden nights and days
    They sang their Elfin roundelays.
The world and we were in our prime
Once, only once, upon a time.

Has Fairyland for ever flown?
– The darkness falls on me alone,
    For on my sweet companion's eyes
    There shines the light of Paradise.
The heights of joy I cannot climb
As we did once upon a time.

Oh, loved one of the far away,
I know that we shall meet some day,
    And once again walk hand in hand
    Through all the realms of Fairyland,
And heaven's own harps around us chime,
As they did – once upon a time!

If: 1

If I should die tonight,
And you should come,
And stand beside me,
Lying cold and dumb,
And, if while standing there,
You whispered low,
'Here's the ten pounds,
You lent me years ago,'
I would arise, although they'd laid me flat,
And say, 'What's that?'

If I should die tonight,
But rose to count,
With trembling fingers,
That long lost amount,
I might live on;
    But when
You said, 'Here's your umbrella
And your fountain pen,'
For one short space
I'd gaze into thy face
    And then
Drop dead again.

If: 2

If you were but the cover
And I the metal tyre,
I'd hold thee like a lover
And tell thee my desire.
And though thou wert deflated,
I still would feel elated
If thou wert but the cover
And I the metal tyre.

If thou wert but the gear-case
And I the driving wheel,
'Twould seem to thee a queer case –
But oh, what joy I'd feel
To have thee close beside me
No matter what betide me
If thou wert but a gear-case
And I the driving wheel.

The Last London Cab Horse

There's a roaring in the roadway, there's a hooting in the air:
There are taxis flashing by on ev'ry side;
There are mighty motor omnibuses rushing everywhere –
It is time that this old horse died.
I've tried to go their pace, lad, for I've been a 'bit o' blood'
I've tried it for a quarter of an hour,
Then I've ambled on as usual through dust and tar and mud –
An antiquated one horse power.

Now they talk of forty horses — sixty horses it may be –
That never seem to want the whip or spur,
I admit that all these horses are invisible to me,
But their vehicles go by me with a whirr!
For a time I drew old ladies, but I know my day is done,
And though of fancy hacks I was the flower,
'The Home of Rest' at Cricklewood is all that's left for one
Who is rated as a one horse power.

The painters and photographers regret the old 'gee-gee',
Who, harnessed to the harrow or the plough,
'Composed so very pleasantly' when wending o'er the lea –
A locomotive poses for them now!
For how was he to cope with electricity or steam,
And plough eleven acres in the hour?
In legends of the long ago he lives again – a dream;
A memory of one horse power.

Great dragonflies are booming in the welkin overhead,
And hydroplanes are humming round the shore;
Electric trains are whizzing – 'tis enough to wake the dead! –
But the draught horse isn't wanted any more.
This locomotive lunacy may fill me with disgust,
And still there's little use in turning sour;
For why should men who float and fly go crawling in the dust,
Restricted to my one horse power?

Red-Letter Days

I was feeling slightly seedy
When a letter signed 'Mecredy'
Came across the Irish Channel to my home in London town;
And I said in language shoppy,
'Here's the Boss a wantin' copy,'
And my forehead corrugated in a formidable frown.

'Ho! Wagtale, wake from slumber!
 For I want our Birthday Number
To contain a set of verses from thy venerable pate.
 Send me something reminiscent
 Of the days when first we listened
To thy songs around the campfire and we'll pay a special rate.'

 It was not the extra rating
 Sent these waves of thought vibrating
Through the years that lie behind me to the pre-pneumatic days,
 When I rode a solid tyre,
 And thought myself a flyer
If I beat the Allens' pony in a race to Ballyhaise.

 But I always love to turn
 To the feast of good St Hearn,
When with racquets on our handlebars we drank that day's delights;
 How well our wheels would travel
 O'er the Ballyheady gravel,
How good those games of tennis! how grand our appetites!

 I have still a fair digestion,
 But could I – it's a question,
Eat plum pudding and play singles with these stalwart friends of mine,
 Then home by moonlight fly it?
 No, Jack Hearn! – let others try it,
You and I will fight those battles o'er the walnuts and the wine.

 Then the day I went a-wheeling,
 Round the lovely shores of Sheelin,
When the perfume of the Primrose told that spring had really come;
 And I rode my cycle dreaming
 That Beauty's eyes were beaming,
And I'd find cead mile failte in the halls of old Crossdrum!

 Sweet Glenfinlas! I'm your debtor,
 For many a red letter
Must mark the days we cycled by Lough Katrine's silver strand.
 Derrynane! thy sunset glory
 I have painted con amore,
When she and I were members of Mecredy's merry band.

 'Oh, my Tour-alluring laddie,'
 I am now a white-haired daddy;
In an easy chair I'm sitting by a comfortable blaze,
 But my thoughts away are winging
 To the laughter and the singing
And the cycle bells a-ringing in those old red-letter days!

161

The Test Of Courage

I have seen the tiger springing
In a terrifying curve,
I have felt the python clinging
And never lost my nerve,
I've checked the charging elephant
With bullets in his brow,
And only murmured, 'Well, if Aunt
Could only see me now.'
But prove your boasted bravery, and put it past a doubt,
By bicycling down Bond Street when the taxi-cabs are out!

I've faced the fretful porcupine
And dodged his poisoned quill,
And thought, 'If for a lark you pine,
This seems to fill the bill.'
I've sailed the South Pacific
In a swift Peruvian bark.
They tell me I'm terrific
When I'm fighting with a shark.
But to win the badge of bravery, and all your foes to flout,
Go bicycle down Bond Street when the taxi-cabs are out!

I've seen the hippopotamus
Rise swiftly at a fly,
And, cool as if I'd caught a mouse,
I've yanked him high and dry.
I've seen a herd of buffaloes
Come charging down on me,
And greeted them with gruff 'hallos'
That made them turn and flee.
But if about your bravery there should be any doubt,
Go bicycle down Bond Street when the taxi-cabs are out.

To The West

The Midland Great Western's doing its best,
    And the circular ticket is safe in my vest;
But I feel that my holiday never begins
    Till I'm in Connemara among the Twelve Pins.

The bank has no fortune of mine to invest
    But there's money enough for the ones I love best;
All the gold that I want I shall find on the whins
    When I'm in Connemara among the Twelve Pins.

162

Down by the Lough I shall wander once more,
   Where the wavelets lap lap round the stones on the shore;
And the mountainy goats will be wagging their chins
   As they pull at the bracken among the Twelve Pins.

And it's welcome I'll be, for no longer I'll meet
   The hard, pallid faces I find in the street;
The girl with blue eyes, and the boy with brown shins
   Will stand for their pictures among the Twelve Pins.

Tonight, when all London's with gaslight agleam,
   And the Carlton is filled with Society's cream,
I'll be 'takin' me tay' down at ould Johnny Flinn's,
   Safe an' away in the heart o' the Pins.

Sweet Lavender

From street to street we wandered on
   A sellin' sprigs o' lavender,
But all my love o' life has gone
   Ever since I lost her.
Sometimes an echo sounding clear
   Will mock me as I pass along,
And make me think I still can hear
   Her old time song.

We never had too much to eat,
   Too little it might often be,
But life was wonderfully sweet
   To her and me.
I meant to call her all my own
   As soon as I had saved a pound,
But she is gone, and I'm alone,
   Upon my round.

There were no lilies for the maid
   Who lay so peacefully at rest,
A bit o' lavender I laid
   Upon her breast.
The parson says she's better so,
   From care and want for ever free,
But then she didn't want to go!
   And wot price me?

The Islands Of Aran

The islands of Aran are callin' me
   Over the foam
Treeless and barren they're callin' me
   Callin' me home,
Home where you wander along the shore,
Kind to the feet is that sandy floor,
And voices are calling me evermore
   Callin' me home.

Over the mountains they sing to me
   Sing to me –
This is the message they bring to me
   Out on the sunlit sea;
Send us the word, an' the boat we'll steer
Safe as a bird to the Claddagh pier,
Follow yer heart and you'll find it here
   Safe in its home.

Valley an' mountains are calling me
   Calling me home,
Silvery fountain is calling me
   Over the foam,
Isles of the Blest they were called of yore,
Come home and rest by the sandy shore,
Meehaul alanna, we've missed ye sore,
   Won't ye come home?

Things That Matter

Father's lost all the money he made.
   I think it's the best bit of fun;
He says I must go into trade
   And make bricks, like my gran'papa done.

We're living out here in a wood,
   We don't have no pie and no cake;
But, lordy! the fishes are good
   I help him to catch in the lake!

We were going abroad for a spell,
   A tutor had me in his clutch;
And Sis was to learn how to yell
   In French and Italian and Dutch.

An' Mother says, 'Isn't it sad?
   No knowledge we e'er can implant.'
But I'm a lot gladder than glad,
   For I'm learning the things that I want!

There's no grand piano down here –
   How Sis and I hated the thing –
But Sam plays the banjo by ear
   And we're learning to vamp and to sing.

At Christmas Pa hadn't the cash
   For a single mechanical toy –
But as there is nothing to smash
   I'm not called 'a mischievous boy'!

Ma thinks that I miss the small gals
   That look down on us now with such airs,
But squirrels are awful good pals
   And Sam has a parrot that swears.

We've not seen a doctor for weeks;
   Pa looks like a Bowery Tough;
And Ma has got red in her cheeks
   That isn't put on with a puff.

* * *

There's just one small cloud in our sky –
   I suppose it is wrong to complain –
But Pa says he is going to try
   And make a big fortune again.
We'll live in some horrible town
   Where no one knows how to have fun;
And he will be Millionaire Brown
   And I'll be his prig of a son!

But meanwhile our money is spent;
   We've nothing to get or to give;
On schools we don't spend a red cent,
   But we're learning – we're learning to live.

In Exile

This London sky is dull and grey;
   A storm of sleet and rain
Is beating dismally today
   Upon my window pane.
On wings of fancy let me stray
   To summer shores again.

Once more the fresh Atlantic breeze
   Its friendly greeting cries;
Afar across the azure seas
   The cliffs of Achill rise
And cloudland's countless pageantries
   Sweep thro' the sunlit skies.

The distance fills with misty hills,
   Alternate gleam and gloom;
I see again the purple plain
   Bestarred with golden broom,
Whilst at my feet the meadowsweet
   Pours forth its faint perfume.

So when along the Achill Sound
   The Summer sunset gleams,
And when the heather bells are found,
   Beside the mountain streams,
I'll seek thy shore and live once more,
   Oh island of my dreams!

Paradise

Somewhere east of the Euphrates,
    Hidden now from human eyes,
Men tell me that the gate is
    Of an earthly Paradise.

Some scorn the ancient story –
    Vague tales of long ago,
But I have seen the glory –
    I have been there – and I know.

I have found it – I have found it,
    Though now 'tis but a dream,
I know the woods that bound it,
    I know the silver stream.
Sweet thoughts we two were thinking
    As we wandered hand in hand,
And, as the sun was sinking,
    We found Enchanted Land.

She turned to me and kissed me,
    With love light in her eyes,
Oh, wealth and fame have missed me,
    But I've been to Paradise!

Not east of the Euphrates,
    Nor guarded from above,
Ah, no, the Golden Gate is
    Where Love has answered Love.

And high born hearts and lowly,
    May find these fields and know,
The song serene and holy,
    Our hearts heard long ago.

The shades of night were falling,
    E'en then across her way,
She heard the Angels calling,
    She wept – but might not stay.

So when the shadows hide me,
    And darkness veils mine eyes,
Sweet Spirit, come and guide me,
    Once more to Paradise.

Retrospection

A boat upon the billow,
A bird upon the wing,
A boy upon a bicycle
Sailing through the Spring.

List'ning in the greenwood
For redskins in the scrub,
Cows – a herd of buffaloes,
The cat – a tiger cub!

The lonely curlew calling
Meant a maiden in despair,
And the rustling of the rabbit
Was the advent of a bear.

Could I find again the woodland
Where I loved to lie and dream,
While the dragonflies were dancing
To the rippling of the stream.

I'd give up all the world has brought
And all that it may bring,
To be that merry boy again
Sailing through the Spring.

The Arab's Farewell To His Steed

A Modern Version

*'The Arab's Farewell to his Steed' was a favourite recitation in
my young days. On declaiming it recently to my youngest
Hope (so young that there is still hope), she asked me 'What
was a steed?' Under these circumstances I have thought it well
to write an up-to-date version of the above-mentioned
transaction. – W.P.F.*

My motor car! My motor car!
That stands vibrating by,
I've sold thee to a stranger
I have done him in the eye!

A list of all thy merits
I've impressed upon his mind
And to thy faults – though manifold
I've been a little blind.

'Tis he will know the agony,
The sudden thrill of fear,
When skirting round a waggon he
Finds out thou wilt not steer.

'Tis he will take the fountain pen,
And sign the little cheque,
To compensate the widow when
The chauffeur breaks his neck.

'Tis his to turn from sweet to sour
When bothered with back fire,
'Tis his to spend a swearful hour
A tinkering at the tyre.

I wonder how he'll work it
(He's a novice at the art),
When he comes on a short circuit
Or he cannot make a start!

Now he will go a poking,
To find what's gone astray,
And never twig the choking
Of the carburetter spray.

And the depth of woe – he'll plumb it
When on some mountain range,
Just half-way from the summit,
The gears refuse to change.

For me the ruby wine shall flow
In Mooney's pillared Fane
Whilst he is cursing high and low
The snapping of the chain.

Every bee that's in thy bonnet
Thy purchaser will know,
So thou mayst depend upon it
I am glad to let thee go!

(Exit chuckling)

Jack Sprat Could Eat No Fat
(Done into Lowland Scotch by Rabbie Burns)

Ye ken the tale o' guid man Sprat,
Wha couldna eat a bit o' fat,
But then his wife made up for that,
    So 'twas nae matter.

What she could eat Jock wouldna hae
And sae the vittles passed away,
The dog and cat the neighbours say
    Found empty platter.

Little Jack Horner
(In the Byronic Style)

– Within a windowed niche of that high Hall
Sat little Johnny Horner; he did hear
His hungry comrades from the playground call,
And when they bade him share his Christmas cheer
He met their plaint with cold derisive sneer,
Then smiled a smile on seeing them so glum,
Which stretched his gaping mouth from ear to ear:
With callous finger and remorseless thumb
He seized and ate the sole remaining plum.

Tom Tom The Piper's Son Stole A Pig And Away He Run

(Enlarged by George Sims)

How did I win that prize pig Sir
And a beautiful bride as well
Ah that's a bit of a story
As Nance there loves to tell.
Sit down in the easy chair Sir
And I'll tell ye how it begun
With Tom the son of the Piper
We called him the Piper's son.

Some of you lads may remember
The Winter of Forty-nine,
When cows were a pound a bushel
And you got your own price for swine.
And the finest pig in the village
The one with the curliest tail
Was owned by sweet Nancy Simmonds.
Nancy the Pride of the Vale.

Well Tom got engaged to Nancy
Though he didn't care a fig
For her blooming youth and beauty,
But he pined for that peerless pig.
The wedding day came round Sir,
The Church was filled to the brim,
'It wor shameful o' Tom to be late' we said
'With the bride a-waitin' for him'

When over the sound of the bells lads
And over the organ peals –
Straight from the cottage of Nancy
There came some awful squeals –
Tom was stealing the pig lads!
In a moment I saw it all –
I was outside that Church in a jiffy
They tell me I went through the wall.

But battered and bruised and broken
I kept on the robber's trail
Till I laid young Tom by the heels lads
And had that pig by the tail!
And then – I remember no more lads –
I fainted – you understand
When I woke she was bending above me
– And the pig was licking my hand.

For weeks I hung in the balance
Whether to call her mine
Or to put in a claim for Salvage
And collar the blooming swine.
But she said 'Jack we've never been parted
It's been with me all my life'.
So that's how I married the pig Sir –
I mean – How I won my wife!!

Edgar Allan Poe's Suggestion For Jack and Jill

Long ago into the mountains
Where the ever-flowing fountains
Sparkle in the summer sunshine
As they did in days of yore,
Sparkle as in days of yore,
Came fair Jill, the Farmer's daughter,
Came to fetch a pail of water,
And her lover Jack besought her
He might bear the pail she bore,
Bear it now and evermore.

Ere the low reply was spoken
Jack fell down, his head was broken,
And the pail, of toil the token,
Rolled relentlessly before –
Rolled with raucous din before.
Short was Jill's untimely laughter,
For we find her tumbling after,
And on wings of rhyme we waft her
Through the nursery ever more –
Only this, there's nothing more.

Handlebar

By Sir Walter's Caught

Oh, young Handlebar has come out of his shell,
And on his high cycle he looks quite a swell;
Said he, 'I'll run down to the country incog.,
And give myself out as no end of a dog.'
So thus, quite the bright and particular star
Of the villagers' feast, was the young Handlebar.

'Lead me home to thy father,' young Handlebar cried,
'His consent I would crave, 'ere I call you my bride.'
So onward they went till together they came,
To the home of her sire, Pentagonal Frame,
And then introduced her papar and mamar,
To her ardent adorer, the young Handlebar.

The young men and maidens ride high in the swing,
Or to the swift roundabouts fearlessly cling,
But none were so merry, or sent the swing higher,
Than young Handlebar and the fair Rubber Tyre –
'Oh, get away closer! you are, yes, you are',
Thus murmured the maiden to young Handlebar.

Next evening, when Handlebar dropped in to tea,
The very first person he happened to see
Was his wife and his child, who had followed his track,
And came there determined on bringing him back,
And the child, when requested, said 'That's my papar.'
'I think I'll retire,' said young Handlebar.

'You're after my daughter,' Pentagonal said,
'I see you're a gentleman born and bred,
So drop in and see us whenever you can,'
Which suited exactly young Handlebar's plan;
But some one was coming, his scheming to mar –
Ha! ha! 'twas the wife of the young Handlebar.

Then the maiden's big brother relinquished his coat,
And said, 'If you stay you'll be certainly smote.'
Then he opened the door and advised him to scoot,
And pointed his words with the end of his boot.
A yell and a tumble, two hops and a jar,
And off on his bike fled the young Handlebar.

His wife followed after by catching the train.
I fear that he found it was hard to explain
But it seems he's so hardened, his chiefest regret,
Is that leaving the cottage his watch wasn't set.
'For the time that I took in returning, oh, lor'
Must have busted the record,' said young Handlebar.

Ride A Cock Horse

Sir Walter Scott's Version

'Ride on,' he cried, nor slackened rein
    Until above the wooded plain
He saw the market-cross again
    That Banbury's burghers made,
And there to gaze on fair Elaine
    His wooden horse he stayed.

In sooth she was a goodly sight,
    She rode a steed of snowy white,
With rings her fingers were bedight,
    With bells upon her toes.
At every movement, howe'er slight,
    Soft melodies arose.

Little Boy Blue

(By Henry Wadsworth Longfellow)

Tell me not in mournful numbers
    That the cow is in the corn,
If it is Boy Blue that slumbers
    Let him wake and blow his horn.

If the cow has left the shadow
    Of the tree where it had lain,
If the sheep is in the meadow,
    Let the echoes wake again.

Cows are real – cows are earnest,
    If he does not chase her now,
He will find ere eve returnest
    All the corn is in the cow!

How Roley Poley Would Be Re-Written By
R–dy–d K–pl–ng

The tale is as old as a Simla Hill,
   And yet it is always new,
The tale of the tear-drops that lovers distil
   From the eyes of the women they woo.

He was round, was young Roland, and sturdy of limb,
   Roley Poley they called him in camp,
And the Major's four daughters were nothing to him
   Though they loved him – the red-headed scamp.

He'd ride out with Mary, play tennis with Kate,
   Fair Fanny to fish he'd invite,
And then in the evening sweet Winnie would wait
   For the kiss when he bade her good-night.

Their mother, who knew he'd ten thousand a year,
   Said she looked on him quite as a son,
But when asked his intentions he made it quite clear
   That 'By Jove, don't you know,' he'd got none.

The fish are forgotten, neglected the net,
   The pony is feeling the lash,
And sweet little Winifred's eyelids are wet
   As she dreams of a ruddy moustache.

The tale is as old as a Simla Hill,
   And yet it is always new,
For changing the name of the hero, they still
   Tell the same little tale about you.

Baa Baa Black Sheep
(A la Rudyard Kipling)

(And this is the song of the black sheep,
And the song of the white sheep too,
And the awk and the armadillo
And the crocodile knows it's true.)

'Have I wool?' said the Baa Baa Black Sheep.
'You ask me have I wool?
When I yield each year
To the shepherd's shear
As much as three bags full.'

'Have I wool?' said the Baa Baa Black Sheep.
'Go forth to the frozen zone,
And my wool they wear
Where the polar bear
And the walrus reign alone.'

'Have I wool?' said the Baa Baa Black Sheep.
'Examine the sailor's socks,
Retaining their heat
Through the driving sleet,
And the gales of the Equinox.'

(And this is the song of the Black Sheep,
And the song of the white sheep too,
And they make up this song
As they wander along
And it's not very hard to do.)

Taffy Was A Welshman
(Re-told by Robert Browning)

'That is the bolster, I have hung it where
   You others hang some trophy from the war
Over the mantel – 'tis an old story – Care
   To hear the details of it? – Right you are, –

This Taffy was a Welshman and a thief
   The terms are not synonymous, my friend –
He may by now have turned a newer leaf,
   How runs the saw ''Tis ne'er too late to mend'.

The man was hungry, starving – had no food,
   He knew that I had much to eat and drink
And so he came and stole – you know the mood
   The act needs no analysis, I think.

Then mark the sequel – Taffy stole my beef
   And I, who hold the law's delays in dread
Cæteris paribus stalked my Cymric thief
   And stole the bolster from beneath his head.

He never woke, ah there's the master hand
   To rob a larder – that is not so hard.
If you should ever want some robb'ry planned
   And executed – then, Sir – that's my card.'

Little Bo-Peep

Wordsworth's Version

I walked with her upon the hill,
    Her grief was very deep,
Her tears were running like a rill,
    For she had lost her sheep.

'What were they like, my gentle maid,
    Were they some special kind?'
'They all had heads in front,' she said,
    'And all had tails behind!

'Their bodies were between the two,
    Their mouths were full of teeth,
And – this, perhaps, may prove a clue –
    Their legs were underneath.'

'If they have legs,' I cried with joy,
    'Your tears you may refrain,
For 'tis their legs they will employ
    To bring them home again!'

Browning's Version

Gone! while Bo-Peep in a day-dream was pondering
    Gone! where the grasses were green to the eye,
Over the hills and the valleys a-wandering,
    Scent in the clover, and sun in the sky.

Feel no remorse for them – they've not confessed any!
    Give them no thought as they wander and wind,
Home they'll return – to return is their destiny –
    Tails all dejectedly hanging behind.

Little Miss Muffet

(A Tennysonian Idyll)

Comrades, leave me on my tuffet,
    Leave me to my curds and whey;
Call me by the name of Muffet
    When 'tis time to go away.

Unobserved he sat beside her,
    Dropping from the linden tree;
He was but a beastly spider,
    And the maiden Muffet she.

In her ear he whispers grimly
    Let me share your curds and whey,
But the maiden, rising primly,
    Left the bowl and fled away.

And the spider fain would follow,
    But he thought the safer role,
Was to stay behind and swallow
    All he found within the bowl.

Old Mother Hubbard

(From Professor Aytoun's Point of View)

Come hither, wee Magreegor, lad,
    And stand beside my knee,
I've told thee once of Old King Cole
    And of his fiddlers three.

I've told thee of the fate that met,
    The would-go-wooing frog,
But never have I told thee yet –
    Of Mother Hubbard's dog.

She sought the cupboard for his meal,
    She sought and found it bare,
She little knew the dog could steal
    The bone that once was there.

With simulated grief he rolled
    Upon the cottage floor
And not a quivering eyelid told
    He'd had that bone before.

Humpty Dumpty

(By Bret Harte. Colloquial style)

So, stranger, you've come
To my store for a chat,
An' yer settin' right plum
On the wall whar he sat!
Who sat? Why that cuss Humpty Dumpty,
Haven't they told ye o' that?

Made no sort o' fuss,
While he sat on that wall,
But I guess he scart us
When the fool had a fall;
And the way the King sent out his horses
Jes' showed he was someone – that's all.

Yas, they tried hard to git him together,
With Putty and tin tacks and glue,
But he'd come to the end of his tether,
What's that you say? – it ain't true!
Why you Pumpkin! You sawed-off assassin!
Why Humpty, you horse-thief! It's you.

Tom Hood's Version

Take him up tenderly
    After his fall,
There let him mend or lie
    Low on the wall.

Dropped from security
    Into the dust,
All his white purity
    Gone when he bust.

All the King's Cavalry
    Came to his aid
As on the gravel he
    Sloppily stayed.

Though they may cleverly
    Tend to the slain
Humpty may never lie
    Heart-whole again.

So when we tell of him
    Turn from his fall
Just the white shell of him
    Only recall.

Goosey Goosey Gander

(By various Authors)

Kipling's version

And this is the song that the white woman sings,
    When her baby begins to howl;
The song of the goose and its wanderings
    The song of the fate-led fowl.

The song of the chamber of her whom I loved,
    The song of the chamber where –
I met an old reprobate, scented and gloved,
    And hurled him down the stair.

And wherever the Saxon speech is heard,
    By the pig or the polar bear,
We follow the feet of that wandering bird
    As they wobble from stair to stair.

Swinburne's Version

Oh whither, oh why, and oh wherefore
    Great goose thou art gosling no more,
With none to caress thee nor care for,
    Wilt wander from floor to floor?

Is it upstairs thy Gandership's goal is,
    Or dost thou descend from above?
To where in her Holy of Holies
    Low lieth my love.

Where I met with the man who is hairless
    And holding his left leg in thrall,
Propelled him, all pallid and prayerless,
    From attic to hall.

Ye tentless, feckless, Drumlie Goose,
That wanders oop and doon the hoose,
Yer keepers maun be kind and croose,
    Ye'd raise ma dander.
For weel y'ken ye've na excuse
    For sich meander,
I doot ye've coom to feast yer eyes
Where yonder bonnie leddy lies,
Yer gladsome een yer wa'fu' sighs
    The way ye scanned her, –
Yer no a goose or I'm no wise
    Yer a'a gander.

Longfellow's Version

If you ask me whence the story
Whence the tale and the tradition,
Whence the tale of Goosey Gander,
I would answer 'Ask a p'liceman',
Ask the blue bird the policeman
Wither wanders Goosey Gander?
From its home in Nursery Rhymeland,
Till it reach my lady's chamber,
Where it disappears abruptly
And for ever from my story.
For a man becomes the hero,
Who, renouncing his devotions,
Is subjected by the author
To the most outrageous treatment.
– And I could go on for ever
In this very simple metre,
But the reader mightn't like it,
So perhaps I'd better drop it.

Macaulay's Version

'Twas Goosey Goosey Gander
Had wandered far away,
From the green steeps
Where Anio leaps
In clouds of silver spray.
This week the stately gander sails
Untended on the tide,
This week the yellow gosling finds
No mother by its side.
This week the large-eyed frog may leap
All careless from the foam,
For Goosey Goosey Gander
Has wandered off to Rome.

But in my lady's chamber
Is terror and affright,
For news they bring
Of a fearsome thing
That wanders through the night.
Then spake the boy in buttons
Give me the knife and fork,
And I will assail
The spectre pale,
That wanders through the dark.
The knife and fork they bring him,
He rushes forth to slay,
One wild death cry
And giblet pie
Is cheap in Rome today.

Sing A Song O' Sixpence

(Amended by Omar Khayyam)

I sing a song of sixpence and a pie,
In which a choir of tuneful blackbirds lie:
And when the pie was opened and they sing,
A dainty dish to greet a monarch's eye.

The King was in his parlour counting gold,
The Queen's fair fingers bread and honey hold,
The maid was in the garden spreading clothes
Meanwhile the blackbird pie is growing cold.

So if the King cares not for pigeon pie
And if the Queen heeds not their tuneful cry,
Come then with old Khayyam to some fair mead
And we'll discuss the dainty thou and I.

(As rendered by an Australian Bush Balladist)

I have sung a song for sixpence and been glad to get the tanner.
I have sung it for a bottle of old rye,
And the Billy's merry boiling seems to bring back in a manner
The blackbirds that were singing in a pie.

The King is in the counting house, he's counting out his money,
Whilst I am on the Wallaby alone.
The Queen is in her parlour – as she eats her bread and honey,
Does she wonder where the Jackaroo has flown?

Ah! There's only one remembers – the maid who in the garden
Let me kiss her while I helped her with the clothes.
She wanted me to marry, but my heart I had to harden
When a blackbird came and carried off her nose.

But like the black man's boomerang that having missed its quarry
Flies back to where its fluttering began,
I'll seek my washer maiden and I'll say 'I'm very sorry',
And we'll marry and be happy – if we can.

Carmody's Mare

There's the saddlin' bell ringing! – the numbers are up,
Oh, man dear! I must see the race for the Cup.
Push up on that plank there! hi! gimme a hand!
Oh, man! this is better than any Grand Stand.
There's high fliers payin' a shillin' – an' two
That hasn't the half, nor the quarter the view.
Hi! **Peter!** McGinty! Miginty me son
Come up here an' see the big race bein' run.

– Not room for another? Oh, now you be civil
– Come up here me hero! – An' you to the divil!
Look Peter from here you can see the whole Course
– Ay, call up a policeman, call up the whole Force!
There's the bank an' the hurdles an' there's the stone wall.
An' there's the big water jump, best o' them all.
Who am I backin'? Well, now I declare
I've got all me money on Carmody's mare! –

– Last night it was Carmody gave me the tip
– (You'll be over the rail if ye give any 'lip')
– He told me the ring men were at him agin
To pull the bay mare – but he's riding to win
Thirty pounds if he pulled her! – ay, that's what they said
An' let 'Queen o' the May' come and romp in instead,
But he'll not take their money, he means to ride fair,
An' that's why me shirt is on Carmody's mare.

There's Carmody! gallopin' down on the bay,
There's Dimpsey, the robber! on 'Queen o' the May',
There's Flynn on 'The Firefly' – Burke on 'Red Fox',
There's Mangan on 'Merry-Legs' – see the white socks,
There's Sweeny on 'Swanshot' – There's Major Tom Goff!
He's linin' them up, boys! – Begorra they're off!
Sit down you in front there! well take off that hat,
I'll take off yer head, if ye give any chat!

Where is he, Peter. Well up in the front?
Oh, don't say that's him at the heel o' the hunt!
Ah, sure, I know why he is keppin' her in,
Yer goin' too fast at the bank, Mr Flynn.
Didn't I tell you, that lep is too wide
No sinsible horse, 'ill take that in his stride.
Ah! look at Carmody – Carmody knows
Hop and go lightly an' over he goes!

174

What's that yer sayin' there? – Heavens above!
Was there ever a race where a man didn't shove!
Fall off an' be hanged to you, little I care,
As long as Ned Carmody sticks to his mare.
Where is he, Peter? – the Hurdles! well done!
Now, see him off like the shot from a gun!
Will you sit down, there, I must see the race,
D'ye want the contints o' me fist in yer face?

Where is he, Peter? Oh! the stone wall,
Ah, Mr Sweeny, you're out of it all.
Don't let her race at it! Keep her in check!
Or ye'll break her two legs an' yer own silly neck!
Ah! look at Carmody, sinsible chap!
Look at him goin' where Flynn made the gap.
What's that yer talkin' of? What's that you say?
The race is a mortal for 'Queen o' the May'!

Oh, bedad! look at her, sailin' away,
Now, Carmody, Carmody, let out the bay,
– Slash at her, slaughter her into her now,
'Tis the bay mare that's under you, 'tisn't a cow.
Hustle her, bustle her, drive her across,
'Tis the bay mare that's under you, 'tisn't an ass,
Now, for the Water Jump, grip wid yer thighs,
Rise the mare over it – over she flies!

Look at the two o' them into the straight,
Carmody gains on him! isn't he great?
Now, for a touch o' the spur in her flank,
– D'ye think ye've the lease o' this dirty old plank?
Will ye go home, and take care o' yer twins?
A thousand pounds level, that Carmody wins!
Didn't I tell ye, ye ignorant calf,
Carmody wins by a lingth an' a half.

Didn't I tell it ye, Peter me son,
Carmody wins, an' I got five to one! –
An' now me good people, I'm just goin' down,
Down to the Bookie to get – me Half-crown.

The Four Farrellys

In a small hotel in London I was sitting down to dine,
When the waiter brought the register and asked me if I'd sign.
And as I signed I saw a name that set my heart astir –
A certain 'Francis Farrelly' had signed the register.
I knew a lot of Farrellys and out of all the crew
I kept on 'sort of wonderin'' which Farrelly were you.
And when I'd finished dinner I sat back in my chair,
Going round my native land to find, what Farrelly you were.

South

Were you the keen-eyed Kerryman I met below Kenmare,
Who told me that when Ireland fought 'the odds were never
    fair,'
If Cromwell had met Sarsfield, or met Owen Roe O'Neill,
It's not to Misther Gladstone we'd be lookin' for repeal.
Would have Ireland for the Irish, not a Saxon to be seen,
And only Gaelic spoken in that House in College Green.
Told me landlords wor the Divil! their agints ten times worse,
And iv'ry sort of government for Ireland was a curse!
Oh! if you're that Francis Farrelly, your dreams have not come
    true,
Still, Slainthe! Slainthe! Fransheen! for I like a man like you!

North

Or were you the Francis Farrelly that often used to say
He'd like to blow them Papishes from Darry walls away?
The boy who used to bother me that Orange Lodge to join,
And thought that history started with the Battle o' the Boyne. –
I was not all with ye, Francis, the Pope is not ma friend,
But still I hope, poor man, he'll die without that bloody end. –
And when yer quit from care yerself, and get to Kingdom
    Come,
It's no use teachin' you the harp – you'll play the Orange drum!
Och! man, ye wor a fighter, of that I had no doubt,
For I seen ye in Belfast one night when the Antrim Road was
    out!
And many a time that evenin' I thought that ye wor dead,
The way them Papish pavin' stones was hoppin' off yer head.
Oh! if you're the Francis Farrelly who came from North
    Tyrone –
Here's lookin' to ye, Francis, but do leave the Pope alone!

East

Or were you the Francis Farrelly that in my college days
For strolling on the Kingstown Pier had such a curious craze?
D'ye mind them lovely sisters – the blonde and the brunette?
I know I've not forgotten, and I don't think you forget!
That picnic at the Dargle – and the other at the Scalp –
How my heart was palpitatin' – hers wasn't – not a palp!
Someone said ye married money – and maybe ye were wise,
But the gold you loved was in her hair, and the di'monds in her
    eyes!
So I like to think ye married her and that you're with her yet,
'Twas some 'meleesha' officer that married the brunette;
But the blonde one always loved ye, and I knew you loved her
    too,
So me blessin's on ye, Francis, and the blue sky over you!

West

Or were you the Francis Farrelly I met so long ago,
In the bog below Belmullet, in the County of Mayo?
That long-legged, freckled Francis with the deep-set wistful
    eyes,
That seemed to take their colour from those ever-changing
    skies.
That put his flute together as I sketched the distant scene,
And played me 'Planxty Kelly' and the 'Wakes of Inniskeen'.
That told me in the Autumn he'd be sailin' to the West,
To try and make his fortune and send money to the rest.
And would I draw a picture of the place where he was born,
And he'd hang it up, and look at it, and not feel so forlorn.
And when I had it finished, you got up from where you sat,
And you said, 'Well, you're the Divil, and I can't say more than
    that.'
Oh! if you're that Francis Farrelly, your fortune may be small,
But I'm thinking – thinking – Francis, that I love you best of all;
And I never can forget you – though it's years and years ago –
In the bog below Belmullet, in the County of Mayo.

If I Was A Lady

If I was a lady I'd wear a hat,
That all the street would be lookin' at,
An' I'd have a ladies' maid, d'ye mind,
To lace and button me dress behind.
A dress that was lined with good sateen,
None o' yer bits o' bombazine,
And the girls with envy would grind their teeth,
When they heard it rustling underneath.
If I was a lady – but then I'm not,
This shawl is the dacentest thing I've got.

If I was a lady I'd drive to the play,
An' I'd look through me opera glass and say –
'I've seen this silly revue before,
The leading lady's an awful bore;
Let's all get up when she starts her song,
An' go an' eat cakes in a resterong.'
Then a powder puff on me nose I'd dab,
An' drive off home in a taxi cab,
If I was a lady – but then I'm not,
A pass to the gallery's all I've got.

If I was a lady – a regular swell,
With a hairy boa, an' a silk umbrel',
'Tis me that would walk into Shelbourne's Hotel,
An' order me dinner – 'Some pork an' beans,
An' whatever ye've got in them soup turreens,
Both the sweets, an' a hunk o' cheese,
And oh, a bottle o' porter please.'
Then I'd call for me bill and settling it,
I'd give the waiter a threepenny bit,
If I was a lady – but then I'm not,
– My dinner comes out o' the stirabout pot.
Still there's a lot of show and sham,
Maybe I'm safer the way I am.

The Only Way Out Of It

Oh, girls! what am I to do,
  Me father declares I must marry
Whoever he buckles me to,
  I know he'll be terrible sarry.

John Flynn has a beautiful place
  Which he'll settle on me – may God bliss him,
But oh! the red nose on his face
  I don't think I ever could kiss him.

Of his riches Pat Hennissy brags
  In satin an' silk he would dress me;
I'd sooner be sittin' in rags
  Than let the ould miser caress me.

Ould Clancy has acres o' land
  A horse and five cows and a dunkey
But the hair on his face an' his hand –
  Ach! ye might as well marry a munkey.

They all have a likin' for me,
  But lovers like them I am dreadin',
There's only one boy that I see
  That makes me think well of a weddin'.

An' he is so shy with his tongue
  Tho' I know with the love he is scorchin';
Oh! why can't he spake while he's young
  An' not wait till he's made all his fortune.

Oh, here he comes over the brae!
  He's lookin' so bowld and undaunted
I think if I met him half-way
  He might think of the words that are wanted.

(*Runs off, and if encored, returns*)

Oh, girls, I had to come back
  To tell ye what happened down yonder,
I spoke of the men on me track
  And how they get fonder and fonder.

I told him I didn't want wealth
  But that I was perfectly willin'
To marry a boy with the health
  Altho' he had never a shillin'.

He proposed and I didn't refuse,
  He's the boy I can love and can honour;
I'm off to tell mother the news,
  He's gone to find Father O'Connor.

(*Second encore*)

Ah! why are ye keepin' me here
  When ye know I'm an eejit to do so.
An' how can I marry me dear
  When I haven't a stitch of a truso?

He'd marry me just in me shawl –
  But that wouldn't suit me, begorra,
So now it's good-bye to yez all,
  Come an' dance at me weddin' to-marra.

(*Exit*)

The Queen's Advice To Lord Zetland
Before Starting For Ireland

(As overheard and reported by Larry Flynn, waiter)

'See here, me Lord,' sez she,
'You'll find it hard,' sez she,
'To play yer card,' sez she,
 'So I'll give ye the tip,' sez she,
 'Before ye thrip,' sez she,
'Take yer mackintoshes,' sez she,
'And yer ould goloshes,' sez she,
 'For it's raining there,' sez she,
 'If it rains anywhere,' sez she.
'You'll be met with ovations,' sez she,
'And grand orations,' sez she,
 'So have yer reply,' sez she.
 'All cut and dhry,' sez she.
'Remark out loud,' sez she,
'Yer dreadful proud,' sez she,
 'At being sent,' sez she,
 'To represent,' sez she,
'This glorious land,' sez she,
'You understand?' sez she.
 'I'm not too clever,' sez he,
 'But I'll do me endeavour,' sez he.
'Take a party down,' sez she,
'To Punchestown,' sez she,
 'And give a ball,' sez she,
 'In St Patrick's Hall,' sez she;
'Or maybe two,' sez she,
'For one mightn't do,' sez she,
 'And Merrion Square,' sez she,
 'Mightn't care,' sez she,
'To be goin' to supper,' sez she,
'Wid Baggot Street Upper,' sez she,

'Don't be axin' for ale,' sez she,
 'At yer midday male,' sez she.
'Make a lot of JPs,' sez she.
''Tis a cheap way to please,' sez she,
 'And sometimes an RM,' sez she,
 'But not many of them' sez she.
'Then open bazaars,' sez she.
'Bless me stars,' sez he,
 'That's not much fun,' sez he,
 'When all's said and done,' sez he.
'Hould on, asthore,' sez she,
'There's a thrifle more,' sez she,
 'You know, I presume,' sez she,
 'At the drawing-room,' sez she,
'There's many a miss,' sez she,
'You'll have to kiss,' sez she.
 'That's not so bad,' sez he.
 'Oh, ho! yer a lad!' sez she.
'I mean for to say,' sez he,
'In a fatherly way,' sez he.
 'Go home, ye ould sinner,' sez she,
 'I must order me dinner,' sez she.
'Remember and steer,' sez she,
'Uncommonly clear,' sez she.
 'I know what you mean,' sez he.
 'Betwixt and between,' sez he.
'Up wid the green,' sez he,
'And "God Save the Queen",' sez he.

The Queen's After-Dinner Speech

(As overheard and cut into lengths of poetry by James Murphy,
Deputy-Assistant-Waiter at the Vice-Regal Lodge)

'Now Maud 'ill write,' sez she,
'That I brought the blight,' sez she,
'Or altered the saysons,' sez she,
'For some private raysins,' sez she,
'An' I think there's a slate,' sez she,
'Off Willie Yeats,' sez she.
'He should be at home,' sez she,

'French polishin' a pome,' sez she,
'An' not writin' letters,' sez she,
'About his betters,' sez she,
'Paradin' me crimes,' sez she,
'In the *Irish Times*,' sez she,
'But what does it matther,' sez she,
'This magpie chatther,' sez she,

'When that welcomin' road,' sez she,
'Come up from the shore,' sez she,
'Right over the foam?' sez she,
''Twas like comin' home,' sez she,
'An' me heart fairly glowed,' sez she,
'Along the Rock Road,' sez she,
'An' by Merrion roun',' sez she,
'To Buttherstown,' sez she,
'Till I came to the ridge,' sez she,
'Of the Leeson Street Bridge,' sez she,
'An' was welcomed in style,' sez she,
'By the beautiful smile,' sez she,
'Of me Lord Mayor Pile,' sez she.
('Faith, if I done right,' sez she,
'I'd make him a knight,' sez she.)
'Well, I needn't repeat,' sez she,
'How they cheered in each street,' sez she,
'Till I came to them lads,' sez she,
'Them "undergrads",' sez she,
'Indeed, an' indeed,' sez she,
'I've had many a God-speed,' sez she,
'But none to compare,' sez she,
'Wid what I got there,' sez she.
'Now pass the jug,' sez she,
'And fill up each mug,' sez she,
'Till I give ye a toast,' sez she,

'Me loving subjects,' sez she,
'Here's me best respects,' sez she,
'An' I'm proud this day,' sez she,
'Of the illigant way,' sez she,
'Ye gave me the hand,' sez she,
'Whin I came to land,' sez she,
'There was some people said,' sez she,
'They was greatly in dread,' sez she,
'I'd be murthered or shot,' sez she,
'As like as not,' sez she,
'But 'tis mighty clear,' sez she,
''Tis not over here,' sez she,
'I have cause to fear,' sez she.
''Tis them Belgiums,' sez she,
'That's throwin' bombs,' sez she

'And scarin' the life,' sez she,
'Out o' me son and his wife,' says she,
'But in these parts,' sez she,
'They have warrum hearts,' sez she,
'And they like me well,' sez she,
'Barrin' Anna Parnell,' sez she,
'I dunno, Earl,' sez she,
'What's come to the girl,' sez she,
'And that other wan,' sez she,
'That Maud Gonne,' sez she,
'Dhressin' in black,' sez she,
'To welcome me back,' sez she;
'Though I don't care,' sez she,
'What they wear,' sez she,
'An' all that gammon,' sez she,
'About me bringin' famin,' sez she.
'At which you may boast,' sez she.
'I've a power o' sons,' sez she,
'All sorts of ones,' sez she,
'Some quiet as cows,' sez she,
'Some always in rows,' sez she,
'An' the one gives most trouble,' sez she,
'The mother loves double,' sez she,
'So drink to the min,' sez she;
'That have gone in to win,' sez she,
'And are clearin' the way,' sez she,
'To Pretoria to-day,' sez she,
'In the Gap o' Danger,' sez she,
'There's a Connaught Ranger,' sez she,
'An' somewhere near,' sez she,
'Is a Fusilier,' sez she,
'An' the Inniskillings not far,' sez she,
'From the Heart o' the War,' sez she,
'An' I'll tell you what,' sez she,
'They may talk a lot,' sez she,
'And them Foreign Baboons,' sez she,
'May draw their cartoons,' sez she,
'But what they can't draw,' sez she,
'Is the Lion's claw,' sez she,
'And before our flag's furled,' sez she,
'We'll own the wurruld,' sez she.

The First Lord Lieutenant

An historical sketch

As related by Andrew Geraghty (philomath)

'Essex', said Queen Elizabeth, as the two of them sat at breakwhist in the back parlour of Buckingham Palace; 'Essex, me haro, I've got a job that I think would suit you. Do you know where Ireland is?'

'I'm no great fist at jografy,' says his Lordship, 'but I know the place you mane. Population, three million; exports, emigrants.'

'Well,' says the Queen, 'I've been reading the *Dublin Evening Mail*, and the *Telegraft*, for some time back, and sorra one o' me can get at the troot o' how things is goin', for the leadin' articles is as contradictory as if they wor husband and wife.'

'That's the way wid papers all the world over,' says Essex. 'Columbus told me it was the same in Amirikay when he was there, abusin' and contradictin' each other at every turn – it's the way they make their livin'. Thrubble you for an egg spoon.'

'It's addled they have me betune them,' says the Queen. 'Not a know I know what's going on. So now what I want you to do is to run over to Ireland, like a good fella, and bring me word how matters stand.'

'Is it me?' says Essex, leppin' up off his chair. 'It's not in airnest ye are, ould lady. Sure it's the hoight of the London season. Everyone's in town, and Shake's new fairy piece, *The Midsummer's Night Mare*, billed for next week.'

'You'll go when yer told,' says the Queen, fixin' him with her eye, 'if you know which side yer bread's buttered on. See here, now,' says she, seein' him chokin' wid vexation and a slice of corned beef, 'you ought to be as pleased as Punch about it, for you'll be at the top of the walk over there as vice-regent representin' me.'

'I ought to have a title or two,' says Essex, pluckin' up a bit. '"His Gloriosity of Great Panjanthrum", or the like o' that.'

'How would "His Excellency the Lord Lieutenant of Ireland" strike you?' says Elizabeth.

'First class,' cries Essex. 'Couldn't be betther; it doesn't mean much, but it's allitherative, and will look well below the number on me hall door.'

Well, boys, it didn't take him long to pack his clothes and start away for the Island o' Saints. It took him a good while to get there though, through not knowing the road; but by means of a pocket compass and a tip to the steward, he was landed at last contagious to Dalkey Island.

Going up to an ould man who was sitting on a rock he took off his hat and says he:

'That's grand weather we're havin'?'

'Good enough for the times that's in it,' says the ould man, cockin' one eye at him.

'Any divarshan goin' on?' says Essex.

'You're a stranger in these parts, I'm thinkin', says the ould man, 'or you'd know this was a "band night" in Dalkey.'

'I wasn't aware of it,' says Essex. 'The fact is,' says he, 'I only landed from England just this minute.'

'Aye,' says the old man, bitterly, 'it's little they know about us over there. I'll howld you,' says he, with a slight thrimble in his voice, 'that the Queen herself doesn't know there's to be fireworks in the Sorrento Gardins this night.'

Well, whin Essex heard that, he disremembered entirely that he was sent over to Ireland to put down rows and ructions, and haway wid him to see the fun and flirt with all the pretty girls he could find.

And he found plenty of them – thick as bees they were, and each one as beautiful as the day and the morra.

He wrote two letters home next day – one to Queen Elizabeth and the other to Lord Montaigle, a play-boy like himself.

I'll read you the one to the Queen first.

Dame Street,
April 16, 1599.

Fair Enchantress,

I wish I was back in London, baskin' in your sweet smiles and listenin' to your melodious voice once more. I got the consignment of men and the Post Office order all right. I was out all morning looking for the inimy, but sorra a taste of Hugh O'Neill or his men can I find. A policeman at the corner of Nassau Street told me they were hiding in Wicklow. So I am making up a party to explore the Dargle on Easther Monda. The girls here are as ugly as sin, and every minite of the day I do be wishing it was your good-looking self I was gazin' at instead of these ignorant scarecrows.

Hoppin' soon to be back in ould England, I remain, your loving subjec,

Essex.

P.S. – I hear Hugh O'Neill was seen on the top of the Donnybrook tram yesterday mornin'. If I have any luck the head'll be off him before you get this. – E.

The other letter read this way.

Dear Monty,

This is a great place all out. Come over here if you want fun.

183

Divil such play-boys ever I seen, and the girls — oh, don't be talkin' — 'pon me secret honour you'll see more loveliness at a tay and supper ball in Ra'mines than there is in the whole of England. Tell Ned Spenser to send me a love-song to sing to a young girl who seems taken wid my appearance. Her name's Mary, and she lives in Dunleary, so he oughtent to find it hard.

I hear Hugh O'Neill's a terror, and hits a powerful welt, especially when you're not lookin'. If he tries any of his games on wid me, I'll give him in charge. No brawling for yours truly,

Essex.

Well, me bould Essex stopped for odds of six months in Dublin, purtending to be very busy subjugatin' the country, but all the time only losin' his time and money without doin' a hand's turn, and doin' his best to avoid a ruction with 'Fightin' Hugh'.

If a messenger came in to tell him that O'Neill was campin' out on the North Bull, Essex would up stick and away for Sandycove, where, after draggin' the Forty-foot Hole, he'd write off to Elizabeth, sayin' that, 'owing to their suparior knowledge of the county, the dastard foe had once more eluded him.'

The Queen got mighty tired of these letters, especially as they always ended with a request to send stamps by return, and told Essex to finish up his business, and not to be makin' a fool of himself.

'Oh, that's the talk, is it?' says Essex. 'Very well, me ould sauce-box' (that was the name he had for her ever since she gev him the clip on the ear for turnin' his back on her). 'Very well, me ould sauce-box,' says he, 'I'll write off to O'Neill this very minit, and tell him to send in his lowest terms for peace at ruling prices.' Well, the treaty was a bit of a one-sided one.

The terms proposed were:

1. Hugh O'Neill to be King of Great Britain.
2. Lord Essex to return to London and remain there as Viceroy of England.
3. The O'Neill family to be supported by Government, with free passes to all theatres and places of entertainment.
4. The London markets to buy only from Irish dealers.
5. All taxes to be sent in stamped envelope, directed to H.O'Neill, and marked 'Private'. Cheques crossed and made payable to H.O'Neill. Terms cash.

Well, if Essex had had the sense to read through this treaty, he'd have seen it was of too graspin' a nature to pass with any sort of a respectable sovereign, but he was that mad that he just stuck the document in the pocket of his pot-metal overcoat, and haway wid him hot foot for

184

England.

'Is the Queen within?' says he to the butler when he opened the door of the palace. His clothes was that dirty and disorthered wid travellin' all night, and his boots that muddy, that the butler was for not littin' him in at first go-off. So says he very grand:

'Her Meejisty is abow stairs, and can't bee seen till she'd had her brekwish.'

'Tell her the Lord Liftinant of Oirland desires an enterview,' says Essex.

'Oh, beg pardon, me lord,' says the butler, steppin' to one side. 'I didn't know 'twas yourself was in it; come inside, sir; the Queen's in the dhrawin' room.'

Well, Essex leps up the stairs, and into the dhrawin' room wid him, muddy boots and all; but no sight of Elizabeth was to be seen.

'Where's your missus?' says he to one of the maids of honour that was dustin' the chimbley-piece.

'She's not out of her bed yet,' says the maid, with a toss of her head; 'but if you write your message on the slate beyant, I'll see –' but before she had finished, Essex was up the second flight and knockin' at the Queen's bedroom door.

'Is that the hot wather?' says the Queen.

'No, it's me – Essex. Can you see me?'

'Faith, I can't,' says the Queen. 'Howld on till I draw the bed curtains. Come in, now,' says she, 'and say your say, for I can't have you stoppin' long, you young Lutharian.'

'Bedad, yer Majesty,' says Essex, droppin' on his knees before her (the delutherer he was), 'small blame to me if I am a Lutharian, for you have a face on you that would charum a bird off a bush.'

'Hold your tongue, you young reprobate,' says the Queen, blushing up to her curl papers wid delight, 'and tell me what improvements you med in Ireland.'

'Faith I taught manners to O'Neill,' cries Essex.

'He had a bad masther then,' says Elizabeth, looking at his dirty boots; 'couldn't you wipe yer feet before ye desthroyed me carpets, young man?'

'Oh, now,' says Essex, 'is it wastin' me time shufflin' about on a mat you'd have me, when I might be gazin' on the loveliest faymale the world ever saw.'

'Well,' says the Queen, 'I'll forgive you this time, as you've been so long away, but rimimber in future, that Kidderminster isn't oilcloth. Tell me,' says she, 'is Westland Row Station finished yet?'

'There's a side wall or two wanted yet, I believe,' says Essex.

'What about the Loop Line?' says she.

'Oh, they're gettin' on with that,' says he, 'only some people think the girders is a disfiguremint to the city.'

'Is there any talk about the esplanade from Sandycove to Dunlary?'

'There's talk about it, but that's all,' says Essex, ''twould be an odious fine improvement to house property, and I hope they'll see to it soon.'

'Sorra much you seem to have done beyant spending me men and me money. Let's have a look at that threaty I see stickin' out of your pocket.'

Well, when the Queen read the terms of Hugh O'Neill, she just gave him one look, and jumping from off the bed, put her head out of the window, and called out to the policeman on duty – 'Is the Head below?'

'I'll tell him you want him, ma'am,' says the policeman.

'Do,' says the Queen.

'Hullo,' says she, as a slip of paper dropped out of the dispatches. 'What's this! "Lines to Mary". Ho! ho! me gay fella, that's what you've been up to, is it?'

> Mrs. Brady's
> A widow lady,
> And she has a charming daughter I adore;
> She's such a darlin'
> She's like a starlin',
> And in love with her I'm getting more and more.
> Her name is Mary,
> She's from Dunlary;
> And her mother keeps a little candy store.

'That settles it,' says the Queen. 'It's the gaoler you'll serenade next'.

When Essex heard that, he thrimbled so much that the button of his cuirass shook off and rowled under the dressin' table.

'Arrest that man!' says the Queen when the Head-constable came to the door. 'Arrest that thrater,' says she, 'and never let me set eyes on him again.'

And, indeed, she never did, for soon after that he met with his death from the blow of an axe he got when he was standin' on Tower Hill.

My Friend Finnegan

When an artist goes to sketch in the West of Ireland, there is often trouble in getting a suitable place to stay in. There are lodgings that advertise bed and board for five shillings, but you can't tell very often which is the bed and which is the board.

Generally, I put in a night at Peter Finnegan's Hotel. Peter is an important man in the locality, and a great friend of mine, and though his four poster bed is really a tripod, and wants the least taste of the window sill to make it a permanent structure, and though by long usage the hens have established a right of way through the coffee room, these little drawbacks count for nothing; for Peter to me is a permanent joy.

'Did you ever remark,' he said to me one day, 'that the three best drinks are in one syllable? Well, it's a fact – port, clar't, and spirits.'

We were looking out of the window at a new house being built, when Peter commented:

''Twould be a great addition to that house, if that gable was taken away.'

He certainly has a quaint way of putting things.

Finnegan runs the hotel on lines of his own. The bells generally don't work; if you want to attract attention you have to go out and throw your hat at them. An English visitor, having at last secured a reply, asked for some water.

'There is no carafe in my room,' he said, 'no water bottle.'

'Well now,' commented Finnegan; 'and I always thought a giraffe was a bird.'

The same visitor had trouble the next morning with the boots.

'Look at my shoes,' he said, 'I put them out last night, and nobody has touched them.'

'That's the sort of hotel we keep,' was the answer. 'Ye might put yer gold watch outside, and nobody would touch it!'

Finnegan is now a Justice of the Peace, and has some good stories of the courts. When I was last there, he had just come home from Limerick.

'There was a judge came down there a short while ago,' he told me, 'and after looking round the court he said to his solicitor, "Where's Peter Dillon?" "Lifted his little finger too often," said the solicitor. "And John Carey?" says the judge. "Came in for money an' gave every penny of it to the publicans." "And Luke Flynn?" says the judge. "Sociable old fella," says the solicitor, "went the same road." "An' do ye all die of drink here?" says the judge. "Ah, no," says the solicitor, "about three years ago there was a Christian Brother died o' pneumonia."'

'An' there was another old man,' added Finnegan, 'died from trying to swallow a lump o' sugar. There was a kettle of scaldin' water on the fire at the time, and they never thought of pourin' it down his throat. I told the Doctor about it afterwards, and all he said was that the man was dead enough as it was.'

One day the local poacher, Larry the Trout, came in after dinner in obedience to a summons from Finnegan, J.P., and this was their dialogue;

'Now, Larry, I have four priests coming to dinner here on Wednesday, and what I want from you is a brace o' phaysants and a twelve-pound salmon by Tuesday.'

'Oh, Mr. Finnegan, where in the world would I get the like o' them at this time o' year; shure the water bailiffs and keepers would have me destroyed.'

'Tell me, Larry, is that case of assault the police have agin ye settled yet?'

''Twill be up at the Petty Sessions next Wednesday, sir.'

'Just so, Larry, and I'll be on the bench; I hear 'tis a bad case. I'll be in two minds whether to send ye up to the assizes, or to dismiss the case for want of evidence.'

'Oh, Mr. Peter, ye wouldn't have me in jail for the races of Ballymacad!'

'I would not, Larry, but justice must be done; and the man who wouldn't oblige an old friend to the amount of a couple of phaysants and a twelve pound fish – such a man, I say, might easily be guilty of manslaughter!'

'Oh, now, sir, 'twas a common assault.'

'Manslaughter, I make it, Larry, and that will be me sacrit opinion till Tuesday night, ay, and maybe after.'

* * *

I dined with the priests on Wednesday, and Finnegan informed me, as he passed the cucumber, that Larry the Trout was still at large through want of evidence.

One day I went down to the Petty Sessions court to see Peter dispensing justice. As we went in, he asked of a constable we passed;

'What about that case of larceny, constable?'

'After a fruitless search, Mr Finnegan, all the money was recovered barrin' one pair of boots.'

We went into the court, and Peter disposed himself upon the bench.

'What's the case, constable?'

'Cross summons for assault, yer worship. Dispute about a turf-bank. John Muldoon, of Carrawallen, versus James McHugh and Mary Anne McHugh, both of Coryglass. From information received, I proceeded at the hour of between 11 and 12 a.m. to the house of John Muldoon. I found him in bed, with a towel tied round his head. I examined him for wounds or abrasions, but could find none, excepting where his head was broken in by some blunt instrument resembling, or of the nature of, an iron pot. (Kawk, kawk, kawk!) Put out that hen there! – Gets in thro'

188

the winda yer worship. I told the plumber about that broken pane two months go. I then proceeded to Coryglass. I found James McHugh in great disorder of mind and body; he said he had been drowned in a bog-hole, and could not talk. Yes, sir, his sister could talk – she's a great masterpiece of a woman, sir.'

'Call John Muldoon. Now, John, what have you to say for yourself?'

'It was last Wensda comada –'

'What was that?'

'Eight days ago last Wensda, sir. I was pershuin' a goat of Paddy Pat's down to the Carrawallen bog –'

'Paddy Pat's?'

'Young Pat Meehan, sir. That goat has me persecuted!'

'Is this a case of trespass or assault?'

'Assault, sir, by that outragious combustible of a woman –'

'Never mind how she strikes you.'

'I wouldn't mind, sir, if she didn't strike me wid an iron pot, and me only tellin' her what she was!'

'Where was this?'

'I'm tellin' you, sir. Down at the Carrawallen bog. I was layin' turf.'

'I thought you were chasing a goat?'

'That's what had her mad with me, sir. Ye see, Paddy Pat's her nevya. An' the goat, not knowin' the harsh sort of woman she is, went to butt one of the childer – Maureen she has her called, afther the sister that went to America –'

'Yes, yes – you were laying –'

'Layin' turf – no sir, not layin' eggs – makin' mud turf, sir, when this bombastical ould termagent comes tearin' down the boreen and this lopsided James McHugh, sir, begins kickin' the turf back into the bog-hole –'

'Ye lie!' (Voice in court.)

'Ye did, ye robber!'

'Address the court.'

'Yes, sir, I'll talk to you. I wouldn't be seen talkin' to him at all. So I gave him a shove, sir; yes, it was with the shovel I gave him the shove – I'll tell you no lie, sir – and over he went into the bog-hole. I'd ha' pulled him out, if his sisther hadn't molested me wid her iron pot.'

'Well, Mr McHugh, is Mr Muldoon telling the truth?'

'He's makin' an offer at it, sir, but I'd not say he was an expert. What I sez to him was – "Ye have no right to be takin' the bread and butter, let alone the turf, out of a man's mouth," sez I; and if me sisther hadn't restrained him wid the iron pot, I'd ha' been drowned to a nicety.'

'Well, prisoners at the bar – or whatever the divil ye call yourselves – this seems to me a case of E pluribus unum, aut Caesar, aut mullus, Poeta nascetur non fit, as the law books say, which means that this case should never have come into court at all. One party has the iron pot, and the other has the shovel. Go out now, the two of ye, and settle it peaceable between yerselves, and the survivor – if any – can appear before me next Wednesday. The court is adjourned.'

Though Finnegan is a great success as a magistrate, I think he is at his best when buying a pig. Last time I was with him, I accompanied him to the Market Square on fair day and witnessed a bargaining battle between him and Mr Clancy, of Killinavat. On these occasions, the two sides start at widely divergent prices, and work slowly towards one another.

Finnegan strolled up: 'Morra, Clancy; and what brings you to the fair? That wan? Oh, now, you're not trying to sell that wan? Not this fair, anyway. Well, now, as a matter of curiosity, what have you the audacity to ask for that outrage?

'£5! £5! Hear that, ye saints in glory! An' is it a golden pig from the Imperial ragions of the Aist ye want me to buy, or is that dirty little runt that you brought home from the fair of Ballinasloe? What will I give? – does the hay-rope go wid her? – I'll say 15s. – for bones and bristles. The fattest pig in the fair! An' I thought it was a greyhound! 'Twould look well in the Waterloo Cup. 'Twould not be so long catching a hare – anyhow she'll not catch me. I'll say a pound.

'£3 for the worst offer at a pig in Ireland! What's that. The best pig in Ireland? God help Ireland! £2 10s. would be highway robbery, with intent to deceive by gross misrepresentation, perjury and extortion. What's that you say? An ornymint for any man's fire-side, and fit for any society? Why I can only see her sideways!

'I'll not say £2 5s. That ould transparency! I'd be disgraced forever if I was seen trying to get her home before she dies of destitution . . . I'll say £2. Done! – and done; – Come in, now, till we wet the bargain. Sure don't I know a good pig when I see her. I've had me eye on her this while back!'

190

Select Bibliography

Chronicles and Poems of Percy French, ed. Mrs De Burgh Daly (Talbot Press, 1922).

Dr. Collisson In And On Ireland, Houston Collisson (Robert Sutton, 1908).

Oliver Goldsmith, John Francis Waller 1860 .

The Careys, Honor Rudnitzky (Blackstaff Press, 1970).

Select Discography

LPs by Brendan O'Dowda devoted to the compositions of Percy French:

  The Immortal Percy French, EMI Stal. 1041; Capitol St. 10213 (USA).

  The World of Percy French, EMI Stal. 6026; Epic. BF. 19023 (USA).

LPs by Brendan O'Dowda which include several Percy French compositions:

  Emerald and Tartan, Columbia 33 S. 111 (EMI).

  The Hollow in the Park, EMI Sker 2003.

INDEX

to Titles of Songs, Poems, Parodies, Recitations and Sketches.